Life, Loss, Love

Life, Loss, Love

A MEMOIR

LORRAINE DOWNES

WITH DONNA FLEMING

ALLEN&UNWIN
SYDNEY • MELBOURNE • AUCKLAND • LONDON

First published in 2018

Front cover photograph by Monty Adams. Back cover photographs from top: Lorraine as Miss Universe; Lorraine and Marty on their wedding day (photo by *The Australian Women's Weekly*); Lorraine at Christmas 2017 with (from left) daughter Jasmine, stepdaughter Emma and son Hilton. All photographs are from Lorraine's private collection, unless otherwise credited. Captions for chapter opening images are on pages 334–335.

Allen & Unwin
Level 3, 228 Queen Street
Auckland 1010, New Zealand
Phone: (64 9) 377 3800

Email: info@allenandunwin.com
Web: www.allenandunwin.co.nz

83 Alexander Street
Crows Nest NSW 2065, Australia
Phone: (61 2) 8425 0100

A catalogue record for this book is available from the National Library of New Zealand.

ISBN 978 1 760633 49 3

Design by Carla Sy

Set in 12pt Adobe Caslon

Printed and bound in Australia by Griffin Press

1 3 5 7 9 10 8 6 4 2

This memoir is about the past fifty-three years of my life. All that I have done and achieved in that period has been possible because of the love, generosity of spirit and kindness of significant people in my life. For all of those beautiful people, I am filled with gratitude.

Lorraine

Prologue

The woman sitting opposite me looked puzzled for a moment.

'That's funny,' she said. 'The world knows you. How does the world know you?'

I was having a consultation with renowned American clairvoyant Suzan Saxman, who knew absolutely nothing about my background when we met in 2016. It was interesting that my 'fame' (something I have never been comfortable with) was one of the first things she picked up about me.

While it's not true that the world knows me now, for a brief time more than thirty years ago, I had been in the international spotlight when I won Miss Universe. Millions of people around the world had watched me being crowned back in 1983, so she was kind of right. But I didn't let her know this until the end of our session.

'Are you related to royalty?' she asked as we were finishing up. 'I keep seeing a crown on your head.'

At that stage I had to tell her about my time as Miss Universe. But our conversation before that point ranged over many topics.

'Are you writing a book?' she asked me.

'I am,' I admitted.

'Good, you must,' Suzan said. 'You are so misunderstood.'

Am I misunderstood? I don't know. I do know that when people hear my name, most of them probably think of that shy nineteen-year-old with the fluffy mane of blonde hair who became the first (and, so far, only) New Zealander to win Miss Universe.

While that one event has had a big impact on my life, it's not all there is to me. I've also run my own successful businesses and raised two wonderful children. I had the most amazing relationship with a man who was my soulmate, and I was his caregiver as cancer slowly took his life.

Suzan was spot on when she perceived that I was writing a book, but it didn't come about because I wanted other people to get a better idea of who I am. Instead, I started writing because *I* was trying to understand who I am.

After my husband Martin Crowe passed away in March 2016, I felt lost. I had been his caregiver for three years, and when he was no longer here I had no idea who I was supposed to be. Suddenly there was a big void in my world. Marty was the love of my life—what was I going to do without him? My children had grown up and were off following their passions, so I was no longer needed to be there for them all the time. What was my purpose now?

I have always kept a journal, and during tough times I have found that getting my thoughts down on paper has helped me deal with whatever is going on. That was definitely the case when Marty got really sick, and also after he passed. Writing, for me, was an important part of the grieving process.

And as I read back over what I had written in my journal, I wondered if some of the experiences I had had and lessons I had learned would be helpful to other people. Despite my sad loss, there were many things I had gained, and maybe that knowledge was something I could share.

I had been asked to write a memoir after I won Miss Universe, and I said no. I was only twenty at the end of that whirlwind year and I remember thinking, *I haven't even lived life.* I'd had one big thing happen to me, but that was all. If I was going to write a book, it would need to wait until later on when I had done much more.

When I was approached about writing a book after Marty died I said no again; I was too bogged down with grief. But the offer came with the proviso 'if and when you're ready', and I kept that in the back of my mind.

Eventually I did feel ready to look back over my life and write about it, and doing that became a crucial part of my healing. The words flowed so easily that I felt as if I was meant to be doing it, and Suzan's advice convinced me that I should write a book. I'm the sort of person who trusts in intuition, and my gut feeling was telling me the time was right to share my story.

It has been quite some journey up to this point, and I have learned a lot; although many of those lessons I never wanted to be taught. There have certainly been some tough and challenging times that have pushed me to my limits. But in other ways I have been incredibly blessed. Perhaps by sharing the things that got me through the darker days, I can help someone else who is wrestling with their grief.

I hope that if you're reading this, you do get something out of it, especially if you've lost loved ones. And maybe, along the way, you'll also gain a better understanding of who I am. There's definitely more to me than the girl from Pakuranga who, many years ago, won a beauty contest.

Chapter One

As far as theme tunes go, you couldn't find a better one for our family. If ever my sisters and I are out together, and that Sister Sledge song 'We Are Family' comes on—the one that talks about having all your sisters with you—Sue, Jenny, Carolyn and I drop what we're doing and head for the dance floor. We dance like crazy and hold each other, and if Mum is there she gets up and dances too. It's always a special moment.

I am truly blessed to have a wonderful family. My parents, Lloyd and Glad Downes, had four daughters; I'm number three, born in 1964. Sue is nine years older than me, Jenny is five years older and Carolyn is six years younger. There's a bit of a pattern—it seems Mum and Dad would have a baby, get it off to school and then have the next one.

Despite the age gaps, and the fact that we're all very different personality-wise, my sisters and I are really close. We know that no matter what life throws at us, we've got each other's support.

Our family is the way it is thanks to our parents. Throughout my life, I have had some incredible mentors and role models who have helped to shape the person I am today. The first ones were my mum and dad, who taught me about love, laughter, hard work and finding balance.

We are family: me and my sisters Jenny, Carolyn and Sue at Jenny's fiftieth birthday party.

My parents had a very passionate and strong love for one another, which was evident to us all. Mum was Dad's beloved sweetheart, and after witnessing their marriage I expected that I, too, would find a man one day who would love me the way my father loved my mother.

I have often wondered how Dad coped with being the only man in a noisy household of five women. He had a gentle demeanour and was very calm—he never raised his voice. He was the peacemaker of the family and would navigate a way through any conflicts. We girls always felt loved, and I'm sure if you asked each one of us who Dad's favourite was, we'd all say, 'Me!'

> 'My parents had a very passionate and strong love for each other, which was evident to us all. Mum was Dad's beloved sweetheart, and after witnessing their marriage I expected that I, too, would find a man one day who would love me the way my father loved my mother.'

Dad was a plumber, which was apparently not what he really wanted to do but it was the path he ended up going down. He worked hard to support us all and keep a roof over our heads in the working-class Auckland suburb of Mount Roskill.

Mum was a stay-at-home mother who did the administration for Dad's business and worked hard in our home. All of us girls learned our work ethic from her. She kept the house beautifully clean. We had black and white chequered lino tiles in the kitchen that had to be polished every week; a task Mum did by hand.

Mum was a great cook, who made wonderful meals and kept the biscuit tin filled with delicious treats. The birthday parties she put on for each of us were legendary, with incredible home cooking, beautiful decorations, games and music. She was also an excellent seamstress who made most of our clothes and, later on, when I started dancing, she made me some extremely elaborate costumes. Unfortunately, I didn't inherit her sewing ability; I'm hopeless at it.

What I did inherit though was her love of fashion. She loved clothes shopping and would take us to outlet stores for the items it wasn't possible to make herself, such as designer-label jeans. And on Fridays—late-night shopping night—we would go to a shoe store called Jerrams in Onehunga. They had a table at the back of the store with sale shoes on it, and us girls would go along wondering which of us might be lucky enough to get a pair of shoes that night, if there were any cheap ones in our size.

Mum liked to buy us nice things when she could afford it, but she didn't spoil us in that way. The youngest of thirteen children, she lost her father when she was nine, and her life was pretty tough. Both she and Dad instilled in us the importance of working hard, and they taught us about the value of money. We appreciated what we got, and the work that had gone into earning the money to pay for it, and that is something I have always been keen to pass on to my children. I believe if you get handed everything on a plate then you just want more, and you're never satisfied.

Our family wasn't wealthy, but we were very happy. Our parents spoiled us with their love and their time, and they set a good example when it came to being kind and thoughtful, and treating other people as equals. They also taught us about having fun. Mum would do things like turning the hose on us while she was watering the garden, and we'd run around shrieking with laughter.

Our enormous backyard was filled with just about every type of fruit tree you could think of, and we would pick pears, peaches, nectarines and apricots from the branches to eat straight away, the juice dripping off our fingers. I spent hours out in the garden playing. Dinnertime was family time; we'd sit around the table talking about our day and sharing our thoughts and experiences.

My sisters and I were quite sporty as kids. We all did athletics, and on a Wednesday night we'd walk several kilometres from our house to the Hillsborough Junior Athletics Club, where we'd do our various activities and then walk home. We didn't expect to be dropped off and picked up; we just accepted that we had to walk. I also played netball for a while and wasn't too bad at it, but when I got into dancing I gave it up because there wasn't time for both.

We did a lot of things together as a family. My dad was a talented musician and won the title of New Zealand's top cornet player in 1969. When I was small our weekends were spent attending brass band competitions, which sometimes involved travelling to other towns such as Hamilton. It was a lot of fun, and very sociable because lots of families would go along to the events. Unfortunately, not long after winning the title Dad fell through a roof and injured his hand, and he couldn't play the cornet anymore. That was the end of the brass band competitions.

Some of my happiest and most vivid memories from my childhood are of our summer holidays. We had one holiday a year: on about 22 December, Dad would hook up the caravan to the car and off we'd go to the Domain campground in Mount Maunganui.

Every year, without fail, I would get carsick and I'd be throwing up by the time we were halfway there. It was always a relief to get to the Mount. Once we'd arrived and parked up the caravan, we all had jobs to do. It wasn't a case of Mum and Dad doing everything; we all worked as a team. A roster would be drawn up so that we knew what we had to do each day. It was actually fun doing the dishes in the cookhouse with my dad.

Days were spent at the beach, swimming and playing on the sand. We'd go for walks around the Mount, and after a day in the sun we'd eat potato fritters and drink milkshakes. Sometimes in the evenings we'd go to the hot pools or for rides at the fairground. I remember noticing my older sisters checking out the boys at the surf club. Once when we were packing up to go home, I asked my mum, 'Why is Jenny crying?' It turned out my older sister was upset about having to leave her summer romance behind.

For eighteen years, I went to the Mount with my family for

Me and my cute younger sister Carolyn in the early 1970s. People were always commenting on my long blonde hair.

My first brush with beauty pageants: winning the junior Miss Mount Maunganui competition at the age of around five.

three weeks every summer, and it felt like my second home. One of the best parts was reuniting with the regulars: the people who came to the campground each year from all over the country. We made some very good friends and had some great times.

Among the regular events held every year at the Mount was a beauty contest, Miss Mount Maunganui. Beauty competitions were quite common at beach resorts back in those days—they were just a normal part of summer activities. As well as contests for older girls, they also had the junior Miss Mount Maunganui competition, and when I was about five, my mum entered me.

I don't recall much about the competition itself, but I remember that I won. I figured it must have been because of my hair. I had very curly blonde hair that I inherited from my dad, whose thick, wavy hair had been blond when he was a child. I was told every day, and sometimes more than once, how beautiful my hair was. It didn't seem to matter where I was in public—whether it was at the library, the grocery store or the school dental clinic—strangers would touch it and tell me, 'What beautiful hair you have.'

When I was nine Mum entered me in the junior Miss Mount Maunganui competition again, but this time I didn't win. I decided it was because I'd had my hair cut quite short.

'Right, that's it,' I declared. 'I'm growing back my hair!'

I was a shy child, and photographs of me as a young girl show me with my head tilted to the side. But once I got up on stage, my confidence grew. Little did I know back then that a beauty contest would have a huge part to play in my life.

At school I always wanted to do my best, and I would sit at the front of the class so I could concentrate on what the teacher was saying. 'Diligent worker' and 'works hard' were two phrases that consistently appeared in my reports from Mount Roskill Primary. I enjoyed learning, and decided I wanted to be a teacher when I grew up.

I had a close friendship group, with one best friend, Linda Rae. Most days, I would go over to Linda's house after school so

School days: I tried hard in class and wanted to be a teacher when I grew up.

we could play our two favourite make-believe games. The first involved one of us being a teacher and the other the pupil, and we would use Linda's big blackboard for our 'lessons'. In the second, one of us was a model and the other was the compère of a fashion show. Linda had a spiral staircase in her house and that was our catwalk—whoever was being the model would stride down the stairs to show off the clothes. I loved my turn at being the model. Already, perhaps, my future career path was intuitively being shaped.

When I was ten, Mum and Dad bought land in Pakuranga, way across the other side of Auckland, and built a new house for us there. Leaving Mount Roskill to live in Pakuranga was very sad because it meant saying goodbye to Linda. It was the first time I experienced real heartache; she had been my closest friend and I missed her very much.

I never saw Linda again. Although we still lived in the same city, the distance made it too difficult to get together and I was not encouraged to try to continue the friendship.

It was tough at first, being the new girl at school. I started at Sunnyhills School in my final year of primary, when everyone else had their well-established friendship circle. But I did manage to make new friends, and it didn't take too long before I felt that I fitted in.

Around the time we moved to Pakuranga, I started going to dance classes. One of my primary school teachers had told my mother, 'Lorraine has got a natural sense of movement—you should enrol her in dance lessons.'

So at the age of ten, I went off to beginner ballet classes. Unfortunately, it was way too late. Most of the other kids just starting out were about five, and it didn't help that I was really tall for my age and towered over everyone else. It was pretty humiliating, and not very good for my confidence. Not surprisingly, I didn't stick at ballet for very long.

But when I was about twelve or thirteen, I got the chance to join a troupe called the Julie Cotter Dancers. We did jazz dancing and would perform at lots of different events, including shows in shopping malls during the weekends and school holidays. We even had a couple of appearances on TV, which was super exciting for us.

I really loved performing. At the time I was a huge fan of the American TV show *Solid Gold*, which played all the latest music hits. I would be glued to the screen watching the Solid Gold dancers, who performed live on the show to the hits of the week. I wanted to dance like them, but I knew I could never be a professional dancer—I wasn't naturally flexible enough. Still, being part of the Julie Cotter Dancers gave me the chance to perform, which I was grateful for, and it also helped me to be more confident. I was starting to come out of my shell.

> 'I was still keen on being a teacher and I applied for teachers' training college. When the letter arrived telling me I had not been accepted, I was devastated.'

I continued to enjoy school after moving on to my local secondary school, Pakuranga College. I had a small group of good friends, and grew particularly close to a Scottish girl named Patricia Gillies. I was a some-Bs-mostly-Cs student, and had to work hard to keep up with my studies. Maths was my most challenging subject, so Patricia used to tutor me after school. She went on to become a teacher, and ended up being deputy principal at St Mary's College in Auckland.

When we got to what was then called Sixth Form (now Year 12), Patricia was determined that my marks throughout the year would be good enough for me to get my University Entrance exams accredited, which used to be possible back then. She helped me with my work during the year, and when the time came for my results to be announced she was just as nervous as I was. We sat together in the school hall, listening as the teacher read out the names of the students who were being accredited and didn't have to sit the exams. When my name was called, Patricia was delighted and hugged me really hard.

'I knew you could do it!' she said.

I owed her for helping me to get through, and for believing in me. To this day, Patricia (now Patricia Adams) is one of my closest and dearest friends. I regard her as one of my mentors and a constant source of good energy in my life. She has been there at various stages to bring me light when I have needed it, and I have a lot to thank her for.

I was still keen on being a teacher and I applied for teachers' training college. When the letter arrived telling me I had not been accepted, I was devastated. I was told that I wasn't mature enough, and that I should reapply the following year.

In the meantime, I was fortunate that there was something I could do that would earn me some money. I had been modelling part-time while at school, and I decided to try doing it full-time until I could get into teachers' training college.

As it happened, I never did reapply to train as a teacher, because my life took a turn nobody could have seen coming.

MISS MOUNT MAUN

Chapter Two

Back in 1980, when I was fifteen, my dad and I were shopping in the upmarket Auckland suburb of Remuera when a man approached us. He introduced himself as Max Thomson, and said he was a fashion photographer.

'I think your daughter has great potential as a model,' he told Dad. 'If she wants to do some modelling, give me a call.' He didn't have a business card; instead he wrote his phone number on a dry-cleaning ticket and handed it to my father.

We didn't ring Max and take things any further, but that encounter made me think for the first time about modelling. A short while later, one of my friends from the Julie Cotter Dancers, Angela Dunn, asked me to be a hair model in a fashion show. It was for a hair salon owned by her father, Murray, and sounded like an exciting opportunity, so I said yes. (Angela is a stunning redhead who went on to become a top international photographic and catwalk model, based in London.)

The salon was co-owned by Di Leaming, who used to compère fashion shows all over New Zealand, and she was the person who really got me into modelling. Back in the eighties, fashion shows were common, not just something that happened as part of Fashion Week. Often they were free public events at shopping malls, or they were held to raise money for various causes.

Later on, when I was modelling in a fashion show at my school, former model Susan Rogers-Allan, who owned her own agency, approached me after the event.

'You did really well—would you be interested in joining my agency and doing some part-time modelling?' she asked.

It seemed like a good way of earning extra pocket money, so I agreed. Susan produced fashion shows as well as running her agency, and she helped to train me in all aspects of modelling: from doing my hair and make-up through to how to walk on a catwalk. I was very grateful for her help.

I was still very shy by nature, but somehow that self-consciousness vanished as soon as I got up on a catwalk. My dance experience might have had something to do with it; this was another kind of performing. Whatever the reason, the catwalk felt like it was where I was meant to be.

'I was still very shy by nature, but somehow that self-consciousness vanished as soon as I got up on a catwalk . . . the catwalk felt like it was where I was meant to be.'

I also did photographic shoots, and one of my first ones was for Pickaberry T-shirts, with well-known Auckland photographer John Daley. We had an instant rapport, and he mentioned he was looking for an assistant to work part-time in his studio.

'What do you think, would you like to come and work for me?'

I was keen, so after school I'd rush over to his studio in my school uniform and help him out with anything and everything, from cleaning up to running errands. He was a lovely man, and he took me under his wing.

One day he said, 'Lorraine, here's your job for this week. Can you please go up into the attic and sort out everything up there—it's a big mess.'

He was right: it was a mess, with props and all kinds of stuff that had been used on shoots lying about. Part of the upstairs area was open to the studio below, and you had to walk on a

My early days in modelling: a series of beach looks for Jennifer Dean Swimwear.

plank to cross from one part to another. I started tidying up, picking up two pots of paint to move them out of the way. But as I walked across the plank with the paint, I lost my footing and dropped one of the pots. Yellow paint went everywhere—all over the lights and whatever was being shot in the studio below at the time.

It was an absolute disaster, and I burst into tears. But John didn't yell or get angry.

'Lorraine, it's okay. It was an accident,' he said.

I must have cost him thousands of dollars in ruined equipment, but he stayed calm because he could see how upset I was.

I learned a valuable lesson that day. Seeing the way John handled the situation made me realise that there is no point in losing it over something bad that's happened, especially when no harm was intended. You can't turn the clock back and change things, but you can decide how you respond to them. Losing your temper achieves nothing. I have always tried to remember that.

We would laugh about the yellow spots that could be found all over the studio. They were still there years later, and John told me every time he saw one of them, he'd think of me.

A couple of years after the incident, when I was preparing to compete in Miss Universe, John said to me, 'You're going to win, Lorraine.'

'No, I am not! I don't have a chance.'

'Trust me, you're going to win,' he replied. 'I'm sure of it.'

When I did win, John sent me a telegram. It said: *I told you so!*

When I was turned down for teachers' training college, Susan Rogers-Allan told me she believed I could model full-time. At that stage only a few girls in New Zealand were earning a living from modelling, and it was risky, but I had nothing to lose. I took the plunge and set about trying to get as much work as possible.

I continued my part-time job as John's assistant for a while, but as I got offered more and more modelling work I had to give that up because I was too busy.

Behind the scenes at a Jennifer Dean shoot. The photographer Roy Emerson is facing the camera. Photo from the Roy Emerson collection.

The modelling jobs I got were commercial rather than editorial—editorial modelling required an edgier look and was where you would find the big 'names'. But this was the early eighties, when everyone was going mad over Farrah Fawcett, and fortuitously I had that American-style, girl-next-door look. I modelled in campaigns for various clothing ranges and swimwear. One of the best jobs I did was a shoot for Jennifer Dean Swimwear at Pakiri beach, north of Auckland. I got to work with another great photographer, Roy Emerson, and being on the beach all day in swimwear felt natural for me after all those summer holidays at Mount Maunganui.

Getting to do TV commercials was also quite exciting. My first one was an ad for a French chewing gum, which screened on television in Europe. I also did one for the Nissan Sunny car, in which I had to speak. My line was, 'I need it!'

It was great fun modelling different products, but my favourite work was still fashion shows. There was something exciting about being a catwalk model—I loved the buzz it gave me. We had to do our own hair and make-up for many of the jobs, and sometimes we even had to provide our own shoes and accessories. To me it never felt like work: it was something I enjoyed and always looked forward to. Even the rehearsals were a lot of fun. And when it came to doing the actual shows, there would be a huge sense of anticipation as we waited backstage. The lights would go down, the audience chatter would dwindle until there was absolute stillness, the music would start and then out we would come. Hitting the catwalk was exhilarating, and I felt incredibly at ease, despite my shyness.

At one parade in Auckland, I was gliding down the catwalk when I spotted a very good-looking young man in the audience, leaning up against a wall and watching me. Our eyes met for a moment. That was my first encounter with Richard Collins, who would go on to become my first boyfriend, and my first love.

Around this time, while I was on holiday at the Mount with my family, I entered the Miss Mount Maunganui competition and won. My prize was a trip to Nouméa, and I went with a girlfriend. At age eighteen I had never been out of New Zealand

All smiles on the podium
after being named Miss
Mount Maunganui.

before, so it was a big deal for me. Coming first also meant that I qualified for the Miss Bay of Plenty contest. This time I came second; I was later told by someone with inside knowledge that I hadn't won because I was from Auckland rather than the Bay of Plenty. Apparently they wanted a local winner.

When the international modelling contest Face of the 80s held its first-ever competition in New Zealand, I entered in the hope that it would help my modelling career. The winner would get the chance to represent New Zealand at the world Face of the 80s competition in New York, for which the top prize was a lucrative contract with Ford Models.

There were only five finalists in the New Zealand competition, and everyone kept telling me, 'You're going to win.' So I got my hopes up, and when the winner's name was read out and it wasn't me, I was devastated.

Katie Ford from Ford Models had chosen a girl from Christchurch named Kirsty Lay, and I could see why. She was after a photographic model rather than a catwalk one, and Kirsty was not only beautiful but also very photogenic, with striking bone structure. She went on to have a very successful modelling career.

I put on a brave face, but when I got in the car with Mum and Dad to go home afterwards I burst into tears. I was so disappointed—there went my dreams of going to New York. But once again, I was about to learn a valuable lesson: sometimes things don't work out as you're hoping for a reason. And that reason could be that there is something else waiting around the corner.

For Kiwi models, going to work in Australia was the next step up the modelling ladder, and I was keen to try my luck across the Tasman. I needed to come up with some money for the airfare, and entering the Miss Universe New Zealand pageant seemed like a good idea, as all the girls chosen as finalists were paid $500 just for taking part.

My photo was sent to TVNZ, who were running the contest, and I was chosen to have a personal interview with the organisers.

After that, I was named as one of the finalists, which made me very happy—I had my fare to Australia. Whatever happened from then on would simply be good experience for my modelling career.

Miss Universe New Zealand was held in Christchurch, and I spent a week there beforehand preparing for the show. For me, getting to travel to Christchurch, meet the other contestants and be part of a live TV show doing what I loved—performing on the catwalk—was a big deal. I didn't think it would get any better than that.

My experience in Face of the 80s had knocked my confidence, and I didn't expect to win. When they read out the names of the ladies placed third and second (second was Marise Wipani, who would go on to be a Lotto presenter), I was sure I wasn't going to get anywhere. So when I was announced as the winner it came as a shock.

Afterwards, I did my first media interviews. By the time I got back to the changing rooms everyone else had left and gone back to the hotel where we were staying. I stood in the dressing room on my own and, despite the fact that I was on a huge high because I'd won, I felt very alone.

I won Miss Universe New Zealand in April 1983, and had two months to prepare before heading to St Louis, Missouri, for the Miss Universe finals. All the contestants had to be there for four weeks before the final on 11 July—during which time we would attend functions as well as practise for the televised contest—and I had to organise my own wardrobe to take with me. I didn't really have many suitable clothes so I had to borrow what I could. One of the items loaned to me was a stunning navy-blue, Audrey Hepburn-style cocktail dress of Mum's. She got it when she was young and, luckily for me, she'd kept it. It was very elegant and lovely to wear. But other than that, I didn't have much else that was appropriate.

TVNZ arranged for my national costume and ballgown to be made for me. I was photographed in the cobalt-blue ballgown for

TVNZ costume designer Dawn McGowan puts the finishing touches on my cobalt-blue ballgown. Photo by Fairfax Media NZ / Auckland Star Collection.

the newspaper and somebody commented on talkback radio that it looked like a witch's dress. I was taken aback at the remark but didn't let it get to me—I thought it was a beautiful gown.

Tom Parkinson, who was the head of entertainment at TVNZ and had experience with the Miss Universe pageant, warned me that many of the other contestants, especially the South American ones, would have different gowns for each function.

'They'll arrive with entourages of support people, and they'll have their own make-up artists, but don't let that make you feel inferior,' he told me. 'What is important is that you should just be "you", especially when it comes to the personal interview.'

That turned out to be very good advice.

Tom also helped with practical training. I would go into the

'I was photographed in the cobalt-blue ballgown for the newspaper and somebody commented on talkback radio that it looked like a witch's dress.'

TVNZ offices at the weekends, when most of the staff were gone, and practise walking down the staircase in my high heels, my footsteps echoing through the empty building. I needed to be able to manage the stairs while looking straight ahead instead of at my feet. I really didn't want to trip and break my neck on live TV.

Other valuable advice he gave me was about camera angles: how to make sure I was seen. 'When you are on stage with eighty girls, you don't want to be obscured by the others,' he told me. 'If you can't see the camera, it can't see you.'

When I practised walking, Tom made sure I knew when to give my biggest smile, and when to relax my face. I was very lucky to have him helping me out.

I turned nineteen on 12 June, and left for the United States shortly afterwards. A small group of wonderful supporters, made up of family and friends, went along to the airport to see me off. Everyone wished me good luck. 'Have a great time; see you back home in a month!' they said.

I don't think anyone really thought that I would win. Nobody from New Zealand had ever been crowned Miss Universe. The only person to get anywhere close was Delyse Nottle, who was second runner-up in 1980.

I felt utterly terrified boarding the plane—I had never been overseas on my own, and I knew that going to America to compete in Miss Universe was a huge deal. I kept telling myself that I had been given a wonderful opportunity, and that I was going to represent my country to the best of my ability.

Once the plane took off, I burst into tears and cried most of the way to St Louis.

MISS UNIVERSE

Chapter Three

My ankles and feet swelled so much on the flight to St Louis that by the time we landed, I could hardly get my shoes on. It wasn't a good look for someone representing their country in the Miss Universe competition, and unfortunately the swelling took a couple of days to go down.

But there was no time to worry about my elephant feet; there was so much to take in. I went straight to the hotel, where I was sharing a room with Miss South Africa, Leanne Hosking. Before I left for St Louis, I had been asked if sharing with her was going to be a problem, because of the issues surrounding the 1981 Springbok rugby tour of New Zealand. I said it wasn't, and was looking forward to meeting her.

Leanne was a tall, stunning blue-eyed blonde who was absolutely beautiful. I always thought she should have won. We hit it off straight away and became so close people called us the Bobbsey twins, after the book characters.

The next four weeks were gruelling. Our days included public appearances and photo calls, but the most time was taken up with rehearsals for the live telecast—it took a lot of practice to get eighty-plus young women from all over the world ready for the two-hour show. Every morning at 8.30 a.m. we would have to be on the bus to the pageant venue, Kiel Auditorium, and after a long day of rehearsals we'd go back to the hotel to quickly get changed before heading out to an evening function. Often we

The Bobbsey twins: me and my roommate Leanne Hosking, wearing our national costumes. TVNZ's Dawn McGowan designed my dress, which was made of cream satin with stylised kowhai flowers over the shoulder.

would not return to the hotel until midnight.

The show included a dance routine, and so one of the first questions we were asked by the organisers was, 'Who can dance?' I immediately put my hand up. The fact that I had some experience proved to be very useful for me, because it meant I ended up at the front of the stage.

However, I was at an obvious disadvantage when it came to the functions and public appearances. Just as Tom Parkinson had warned, the other contestants seemed to have a huge selection of clothes. The South American girls in particular would turn up in a different sequinned gown every night, while I had to alternate between the couple of cocktail dresses I had borrowed. There wasn't anything I could do about my lack of outfits, other than to vow that I wouldn't let it get to me.

It was great getting to know the other girls, and after a while we naturally found people we clicked with and formed little groups. I was fascinated to learn about the other girls' countries and their lives, and realised I should make the most of the chance to get to know so many people from around the world.

When you get eighty girls together people expect there's bound to be some cattiness—a word I hate. No doubt there *can* be nastiness and sniping among a large group of females, but I never noticed any of that at Miss Universe. In fact I've come across it more in the modelling world, thanks to a couple of people I've met who could be that way.

Lots of great friendships were made, but at the end of the day it was a contest, and I was aware of that edge of competitiveness in many of the girls.

My strategy was to be as professional as possible; to work hard at rehearsals, to smile and be friendly to everyone, and to never complain. Some days it was hard keeping quiet about how tough it was; it felt like an endurance test. After three weeks I was exhausted, and I wasn't the only one.

Lots of the girls were saying, 'I'm tired, I want to go home. I don't want to be Miss Universe.'

But I knew I just had to get on with it and make the most of the opportunity. Later I realised that the reason for the hectic schedule was largely to see who could cope with pressure, since the demands faced by the person chosen to be Miss Universe would be much worse. It was a kind of natural culling process, with each contestant carefully watched and evaluated to see how she would cope with the relentless grind of rehearsals, public appearances and photo calls packed into the weeks leading up to the live show. The judges were looking for girls whose traits included patience, willingness and obedience, plus an even temper. It wasn't just down to who had the brightest smile or looked great in a swimsuit.

As well as being worn out, I was very homesick after three weeks away from New Zealand. Fortunately, my parents flew over to St Louis a few days before the big night, and seeing them gave me a shot of energy. Having them there helped me to shine again, which was perfect timing as they arrived just before I had my interview with the judges.

When the day of the pageant rolled around, I was understandably nervous and my stomach was churning so much that I couldn't eat dinner. Before the live telecast, which was seen by a worldwide audience of around 700 million people, I said a little prayer.

'God, whatever happens in the next two hours is up to your will,' I prayed. I felt calmer afterwards.

Everything went well in the parade of nations and swimsuit section, and all that practice walking in heels with Tom Parkinson paid off because I managed not to trip. Prior to the show, the chaperone for the reigning Miss Universe had told me that I was her favourite to win, and warned me not to walk in a sexy way as that could ruin my chances. I thanked her for her advice and said I would try not to. I had no idea what a sexy walk looked like.

When the time came to announce the final twelve girls, I thought, *If I get through, I will be very happy*. That was all I wanted—to make the last twelve.

So when my name was called out first, I was absolutely thrilled. I'd done it; I'd achieved my goal. By that stage any nerves I'd had were gone, replaced by excitement. I was having a ball!

I really didn't think I would get any further, so it was a surprise to be named as one of the final five. I couldn't quite comprehend

Top Some of the many friends I made during the Miss Universe competition. I became particularly close with Miss Australia, Simone Cox.

Above Me and Simone Cox at one of our recent catch-ups.

it. During a commercial break, I looked out at the audience and wondered where my parents were. There were about 16,000 people there, apparently. As I scanned the rows and rows of onlookers, to my amazement, I spotted Mum and Dad in the crowd. The fact that I managed to find them was unbelievable.

I was watching them again a little later on, as the final placings were called out in reverse order. Mum had her head in her hands and Dad was sitting very still and looking super serious. I hoped he was okay—he'd had a heart attack about three years earlier, and this was stressful.

> 'When the time came to announce the final twelve girls, I thought, *If I get through, I will be very happy.* That was all I wanted—to make the last twelve.'

Eventually it got down to me and one other contestant: Miss USA, Julie Hayek. Julie had been the hot favourite to win the whole way through the competition.

Photos of Julie had appeared in the local St Louis papers virtually every day in the weeks leading up to the competition, whereas I had only made it in twice—and one of those times, I had my hair in curlers before an event later in the day. It wasn't a glamorous look. (Miss Australia, Simone Cox, was with me in that curlers photo. To this day, she and I are very close and we catch up regularly.)

I didn't realise it at the time, because we couldn't see the scores we had been getting throughout the competition, but Julie had won the swimsuit and evening-wear sections and had the highest score going into the final round. At that point all scores got wiped, and the judges' final scores were tallied up starting again from scratch.

We stood alongside one another as the host, Bob Barker, talked

Negotiating the stage in my emerald-green swimsuit and heels. I was relieved when I managed not to trip.

about how he would begin by announcing the first runner-up, followed by Miss Universe.

Julie was wearing a very low-cut blue sequinned gown by designer Bob Mackie, and she looked incredibly glamorous. My cobalt-blue dress was beautiful, but I knew it was more 'Lady Di' than sexy.

Julie was breathing so rapidly that her chest—which was almost at my eye level because she was much taller than me—was heaving. Looking at the TV footage later (it is available on YouTube), I could see that she was preparing for her big moment; that this was what she had been working for.

For my part, I felt nothing but peace and serenity. I wasn't going to win, so there was no point in getting worked up.

'The first runner-up,' said Bob, 'is Miss USA. Miss New Zealand is Miss Universe.'

What?

That was me.

I'd won.

Those first few minutes were a whirlwind of emotions. I had won—how had that happened? Surely girls from New Zealand didn't win Miss Universe? I was proud to have won for my country, but shocked that I had been judged the most beautiful.

In the frenzied moments that followed the announcement, the sparkling diamond crown was placed on my head and the Miss Universe sash was put over my shoulder. I was handed an enormous bouquet of flowers.

'Congratulations, Miss New Zealand,' said Bob. 'You said that you'd never dreamed you would be here, and here you are. Lorraine Downes, Miss New Zealand, is Miss Universe of 1983.'

I had to do the winner's walk across the stage, and I remember stopping in front of the judges, looking down at them and saying thank you. For some reason, they had chosen me. I couldn't believe it.

After I finished walking the stage, I headed up the stairs to sit in the Miss Universe throne, and that's when things got really crazy. I was mobbed by the other contestants, who launched themselves at me, kissing me (then trying to wipe their lipstick off my face),

My face says it all:
looking up towards
my parents in the
crowd after being
crowned Miss Universe.
Photographer unknown.

squeezing me and grabbing me. It was awful—I almost felt like I was being attacked.

Then the live telecast finished and I was led off the stage, still in a daze. Thankfully, somebody had found my parents and taken them to a small room backstage. I was swiftly guided in there and the door was shut behind me—somebody clearly thought I needed a moment with my family.

As soon as the door closed, I fell into my parents' arms and burst into tears.

'I can't do this,' I wept. 'I shouldn't have won; I'm not the most beautiful girl here.'

I wasn't good enough or confident enough to be Miss Universe. It was a huge mistake; they should have chosen someone else.

My parents hugged me and gently reminded me, 'Lorraine, you have been chosen for a reason. This is a wonderful opportunity, and you need to give it a go. If you are miserable after six months, we will get you home.'

Mum and Dad helped to calm me down, and I thought about their words as I left the room. I would try my very best, I decided. And if it didn't work out, then home would always be waiting for me.

The rest of the night was complete madness. There was a coronation ball, and while the other girls danced and had fun, I sat on the throne onstage having my picture taken with strangers. Next was a breakfast with the judges, which was actually held at about 1 a.m. Most of them told me that I had been chosen because of my personality.

'Your inner beauty shone through,' said one. That helped me to feel a little bit better about having won.

By the time I got back to my hotel room, it was 4 a.m. and I was exhausted. I was looking forward to seeing my roommate, Leanne (Miss South Africa), but she'd already packed up and gone. She left a big red lipstick kiss on the mirror with the message, 'You did it! I love you xx'.

I sat down on my bed and felt loneliness wash over me. Surely this wasn't what being Miss Universe was meant to feel like?

Celebrating my win with
Mum and Dad.

After just a couple of hours' sleep, I was woken up to attend my very first press conference. For some bizarre reason, I had to do it in bed while eating breakfast. I was asked to wear a dressing gown but I didn't have one—fortunately I was able to borrow Mum's pink satin one. I did my hair, put on a full face of make-up and was taken to a suite in the hotel, where I climbed into bed wearing my crown and Miss Universe sash. At 7 a.m. the room filled with reporters and photographers, and so began one of the weirdest experiences of my year as Miss Universe. I sat in bed, trying to eat eggs on toast, while being bombarded with questions from the media.

'What do you want to achieve during your reign?' asked one of the reporters.

'I'd love to travel the world spreading peace among the different countries,' I replied.

Yes, I know, that's so cheesy, but that was my truth in that moment. I didn't mean I was going to try to stop wars; I just hoped that I might bring some light and joy into the lives of people who were struggling in one way or another.

My reign as Miss Universe started immediately, and that meant going to live in the apartment in New York that Miss Universe, Inc. had set aside for the winner. So instead of getting on a plane back to New Zealand, and my life there, I said a very tearful goodbye to my parents at the airport in St Louis and flew to New York.

Overnight, my life had changed. I was no longer just Lorraine Downes from Pakuranga; I was Miss Universe. And I was more than a little terrified about what the next year had in store for me.

Chapter Four

The door to the Miss Universe apartment in New York City opened and the woman on the other side of it grabbed me and pulled me into a big, warm hug.

'Welcome to your new home, Lorraine—we are going to have so much fun!'

That was the beginning of a wonderful friendship with Ruth Romero, one of the chaperones employed by Miss Universe, Inc. to look after me.

Actually, I had met Ruth before, in St Louis when I sat next to her at one of the many dinners we attended in the lead-up to the final competition. At the time I thought she had been sent by the Miss Universe people to spy on us!

It turned out that Ruth's role was to reside in the apartment with me and Julie Hayek, who lived there during her reign as Miss USA. Ruth, who is Mexican, travelled with Julie on her official engagements, and also accompanied me on some of my trips, particularly to Spanish-speaking places. My main travelling companion was another lady, Shoshanna Orley, but it was Ruth I developed a very close bond with. She has been one of the most influential people in my life, as well as a dear friend.

Getting such a lovely greeting from this cheerful lady with the beautiful big smile and twinkling brown eyes gave me hope that I was going to be okay. She also left a welcoming card for me on my bed, aiming to make me feel a little more accepted.

However, it didn't help my confidence when Julie told me that something had gone wrong with the computers and that she

Me and Miss USA,
Julie Hayek, with our
kind-hearted chaperone
Ruth Romero.

should have taken the title because she'd had the highest scores throughout the competition. However, as all of the previous scores were deleted going into the final round, what mattered was the way the judges scored us from then on. Later, when it became clear that a key part of my job as Miss Universe was to show people kindness and compassion, I wondered if I had been chosen because I was able to do that. It was another reason to give thanks for my upbringing.

Julie eventually warmed to me, but it took her a while to get over the fact that I had won and she hadn't. As the year progressed, we ended up having a warm and friendly relationship.

As Miss Universe, I had to live up to ideals set for me by Miss Universe, Inc. After I won, I was given a handbook reminding me that I was no longer just Lorraine Downes, 'but rather Miss Universe 1983, symbolising the young women of the entire world'. Because I now had a public image to uphold, they offered some suggestions on how I could do that.

These 'recommendations' included no swearing, no smoking and no drinking (light wine or champagne was permissible at the discretion of my chaperone).

'Remember again, that even on your own time you are a "public person". Remember the key word in all these matters is discretion,' the handbook advised.

I wasn't allowed to have overnight guests in the apartment I shared with Julie and Ruth, and all visitors had to be entertained in the living room. All other areas of the apartment were out of bounds to guests.

There was a section in the handbook on my sash and crown, which were to be looked upon with pride. 'The sash is not a label—it is a sign of honour and victory, much like a military decoration. Presidents and Chiefs of State in foreign lands often wear similar sashes as symbols of their office.'

The Miss Universe sash added to the 'magnetism and charisma' of my presentation, and was to be worn at all times. The crown, on the other hand, was reserved for personal appearances and

I was encouraged to treat my sash and crown with the appropriate respect.

occasions of 'full dress'. Wearing it was a matter of judgement, but it was suggested that I didn't go to dinners or casual affairs without either my crown or sash nearby.

It was quickly made clear that I was always to be fully made-up and immaculately dressed in appropriate clothing. I had to smile constantly, be nice to everyone I met, never show signs of boredom or unhappiness, always be on time and never complain about working seven days a week, sometimes for months on end.

I had been brought up to follow rules and work hard, and I've always understood that there are times in life when you just have to do as instructed. But by the end of my year as Miss Universe, I was very tired of being told what to do for every hour of every day, and I was ready to have my life back again.

My first few weeks in New York were all about transforming me into Miss Universe and, I have to admit, I did feel a bit like Cinderella. For starters, I was instructed to have my long, fluffy hair cut into a shorter, more chic 'do. Then Ruth took me shopping. I really didn't have anything to wear that was suitable for Miss Universe, and urgently needed appropriate clothes before I headed off on my first overseas trip.

Ruth was in charge of the budget, and decided how much we could spend. Off we went in search of smart dresses and elegant gowns, and I did feel very lucky when I returned to the apartment with bags of beautiful clothes. One day we went to Innes Shoes Salon on Fifth Avenue and 57th Street, and ended up choosing six pairs of shoes.

'This is way too many,' I said to Ruth.

She turned to the salesman and said, 'We'll have two more pairs, thank you.'

To me she said, 'I love seeing your genuine appreciation—I want to spoil you!'

It was a very different experience to buying shoes from the sale table at Jerrams in Onehunga.

Going shopping and being spoiled was lovely, but also overwhelming. While I was very grateful for what I was given, I

Finding my way in New
York as Miss Universe.

LORRAINE DOWNES
MISS UNIVERSE 1983

The first official photo taken of me as Miss Universe. The next ones were worse.

felt desperately unhappy during that first month. I was plagued with self-doubt and terribly homesick. I knew I had been given an incredible opportunity and I needed to make the most of it, but I was having real trouble adjusting to my new life. I wasn't sophisticated and worldly like so many of the people I met, and I felt like a fish out of water.

But nobody in New York had any idea how sad and lonely I was, as I never let anyone see it. My way of dealing with my misery was to write about it in letters to Mum and Dad. I don't know what I would have done if I hadn't been able to share my feelings with them.

My first overseas trip as Miss Universe was to Hong Kong in September, and I found it really hard. In one of my letters home I wrote, 'Last night I went to a cocktail party full of people who didn't speak English. They kept grabbing me and taking pictures. It was so boring I could have screamed.'

It didn't help that the people I travelled with from Miss Universe were all American and I didn't understand their humour. I felt very disconnected and alone, and at times I was overwhelmed with hopelessness. Neither Ruth nor Shoshanna were on that trip; if they had been I think I might have coped a little better.

Back in New York, I couldn't help feeling that I was just a product, with no say in anything. Some official photographs had been taken of me and I hated them. My years of modelling had taught me to recognise the difference between good and bad pictures, and these ones were ugly, thanks largely to the terrible lighting. I was so horrified that I went to see the head of media at Miss Universe, Inc.

'We need to reshoot these photos,' I told her. 'I can't give them out and sign them; I look terrible.'

'Oh, don't worry about it,' she said dismissively. 'They're fine.'

That was the end of the conversation. She clearly didn't care and wasn't prepared to reshoot.

It was interesting that just about every time I handed out one of those photos, the recipient would look at the picture, then look at me, and say, 'Oh, you're much prettier in real life.'

After a couple of months, I was allowed to go home to New Zealand for three days. It was wonderful to be back in my own country, where everything was so familiar, and to see my family and friends again. It was also a chance for me to catch up with Richard, my boyfriend.

When I was in St Louis for the pageant and feeling horribly homesick, I would phone Richard whenever I had spare time. We had long conversations, which must have cost him a fortune because I reversed the charges. During one phone call he asked me to marry him, and I said yes. It was completely unofficial—there was no engagement notice in the paper or anything—and I didn't announce the news to anyone; I had the pageant to focus on.

But after I won, and there was huge media interest in me at home, Richard announced to the press in New Zealand that we were engaged. When the news reached Miss Universe, Inc., I was summoned to the office of its president, Harold Glasser, and told in no uncertain terms that Miss Universe could *not* have a fiancé.

So when I came back to New Zealand for those three days, I had to tell the media that I wasn't engaged. A press conference had been set up, and during my statement I mentioned that there had been a misunderstanding regarding my relationship with Richard, and there was no engagement. He was actually in the room at the time, along with my mum and dad. Although I had warned Richard what I was going to say, it still must have been hard for him.

And while I was telling the media that we weren't getting married, I looked at him and realised that in fact it was the truth; I didn't want to marry him. He had been my first love and a huge part of my life before I went to Miss Universe, but I no longer felt the same way.

After the press conference, my dad pulled me aside.

'Your feelings for Richard have changed, haven't they?' he asked.

'How can you tell?' I was surprised.

'By your face, Lorraine. You're not hiding it very well.'

As the only male in a household with five women, he was very in tune with us.

A favourite photo of me and Richard Collins, my first boyfriend.

And he was right.

I tried to tell Richard how I felt, but he wouldn't give up on me. Throughout much of my year as Miss Universe he would get in touch and tell me, 'You haven't changed—once this experience is over and you come home, you will be the same person.'

But I knew I wouldn't be, and that I needed to move on. I felt very conflicted because Richard had meant so much to me. But it had to end, and eventually we parted ways.

My win at the Miss Universe pageant had been a big story at home in New Zealand, and I was on the front page of the newspapers and magazines and all over TV. People were so excited that, for the first time ever, somebody from New Zealand had won an international beauty contest. I was very happy that I had done something to promote my country to the rest of the world.

> 'It was quite hard to read some of the things written about me. But it made me realise that not everyone was going to like me.'

The people at home wanted to know all about me, and a popular monthly magazine of the time called *More* did an article in which they talked to people I'd worked with. Some of them were brutally honest about me, including Des Williams, a top fashion photographer. He said I was never his first choice as a photographic model, and that catwalk was more my forte (which was true).

'On the photographic side she didn't appear to have the makings of a top model, she didn't seem to emote. But that might be due to a lack of experience, and it will no doubt change in the future.'

The reason I didn't emote was that I was so young—I believe

to be a good model you need to have life experience, and I'd had none.

Des went on to say that he thought still waters ran deep, and I was probably a 'strong-willed person who will be more than a match for the task in the big world of beauty that lies ahead'.

Richard Marshall, one of the top hairdressers of the 1980s, was also interviewed and described me as 'beautiful but not stunning. She would not bowl people over walking into a room because there is no big force of personality. She doesn't say a lot.

'But what is remarkable about her is that everything is perfect and in proportion. She is one of those women who would still be beautiful if you were to shave all of her hair off.'

Richard admitted he didn't think I would win—he liked Miss Switzerland, whom he considered to be a 'dynamic beauty'.

'Lorraine is a natural beauty and no doubt that was the sort of girl they were looking for.'

It was quite hard to read some of the things written about me. But it made me realise that not everyone was going to like me. I had always been a people pleaser who wanted to be liked, but I understood that people were going to have their own opinions regardless of what I did. There wasn't a lot I could do about that, other than grow a thicker skin.

Chapter Five

My three days in New Zealand flew by extremely fast, and when the time came to go back to New York I was in tears at the airport. I would have given anything to be able to stay at home. But I had a job to do, and I didn't want to let anyone down, so I got on the plane and flew back to the States.

Gradually my homesickness eased, thanks in large part to my chaperone Ruth, who got me through the difficult settling-in period. I was able to confide in Ruth as I got to know her better, and she was my saving grace, giving me her love and support. Although my new life was challenging, I started to get a little more self-confident and to enjoy my work.

There were of course lots of perks to being Miss Universe, including the prize package. It was worth around $350,000 in total. The cash portion (about $150,000) was paid to me throughout the year as a salary, but I saved most of it because my accommodation, food, clothes and travel costs were covered as well. Those lessons from my parents about being sensible with money were deeply ingrained, and when my year as Miss Universe was up I used my savings to buy an apartment in Auckland. Later on, I sold the apartment and put the money into setting up a business. It gave me a great start to adult life, and I appreciated it.

The other prizes included clothes, make-up, jewellery, a camera and an Atari home computer, which was the latest thing in 1983.

One thing I can say
is that Miss Universe
always travelled in style.

I also won a convertible, which I sold because it was a left-hand drive and no good to me at home, and a speedboat, which I kept.

While living in New York, I had access to free facials, manicures and hair-dos—when I could make time for them—and there was a chauffeured limousine on hand to drive me to and from the airport. I flew first class, stayed in five-star hotels (often in the best suite), and I met many famous people, from Zsa Zsa Gabor to renowned heart surgeon Christiaan Barnard. It was very different to my life back in Pakuranga, and I got lots of opportunities that I would never have had otherwise. I will always be thankful for that.

But my life was not my own. My schedule was non-stop, especially when I toured overseas, with appearances booked back to back. There was not a lot of time in the schedule for days off; I was lucky if I got a few hours to myself on most trips. And sometimes there was so little space between trips that I barely had time to unpack my suitcase in New York before I was packing it again to go to the next place. One skill I picked up during that year was learning to pack a mean suitcase!

As Miss Universe, I was contracted to Miss Universe, Inc., who hired me out to various companies and organisations for US$2000 a day—a lot of money back in 1983. These businesses would pay for me to attend openings, dinners, lunches, cocktail parties, fashion shows, conventions, trade events . . . you name it, I did it. I also visited hospitals and orphanages, and met heads of state and other dignitaries when I travelled overseas. I even went to the White House, where I met President Ronald Reagan and sat in the Oval Office speechless with fright.

I went to twenty-five countries around the world in that year. Wherever I went, I would be bombarded with people wanting to get my autograph or have a photo taken with me. I hate to think how many of those official photos of myself I personally signed.

Before the plane landed I would head off to the toilet, where I'd do my make-up and make sure my hair looked good and my clothes were immaculate. I would get off the plane in my sash and crown, sporting a big smile—Miss Universe was not allowed to be jet-lagged or look anything less than thrilled to be wherever she was.

I was pretty nervous the day I met US President Ronald Reagan.

Me and my travelling chaperone Shoshanna Orley at the New Zealand Kiwifruit stand in Germany.

My days started at around 6 a.m. with a breakfast, often shared with representatives of the company that was paying for me to be there, or with tourism officials. I would have a big cooked breakfast, and then I would be out for lunch and dinner, so it was no surprise that I put on weight. Not having any time to exercise didn't help either, and after a few months I was definitely heavier than I had been.

I knew I had to do something about it—an overweight Miss Universe is a no-no. So I got into the habit of getting out of bed even earlier in the morning to exercise in my room or use the hotel gym before breakfast, and I chose not to eat every single thing that was served up to me.

Self-discipline was crucial. I had to make myself do things that I would have struggled with in my old life. I found myself 'conversing' with people who didn't speak a word of English, as we made use of facial expressions and gestures. I became skilled at showing interest in subjects that normally would have bored me to tears. I kept that smile on my face and I never complained.

One appearance I made was at the New Zealand Kiwifruit stand at a convention in Germany. I think I posed for about 450 photographs that day with people attending the convention. I smiled brightly for every single one.

I never let myself forget that as well as being Miss Universe, I was representing New Zealand wherever I went. I wanted to leave people with a good impression of New Zealanders. And I wanted everyone I met to go away thinking that Miss Universe was a warm and friendly person. They didn't need to know that sometimes I was feeling the opposite.

One of the best parts of the job was leaving an event or visit knowing that I'd made people happy simply by turning up. As a nineteen-year-old girl from suburban Auckland, it felt so strange that I could do that simply because I'd won a beauty competition. But I had to accept it and try not to think too hard about it.

One encounter that made me feel really good took place on

my first visit to Hong Kong. The trip was a bit of a disaster all up, because I was still struggling to settle in to the role of Miss Universe. I was staying in a beautiful suite at the luxurious Regent Hotel and had my own butler, Thomas. With the push of a button, he would be there to do whatever I wanted. He was very sweet and I gave him one of my official Miss Universe photos, signing it for him personally.

'Thank you, Miss Downes, I will treasure this for the rest of my life,' he said, very seriously.

As he left my room I could hear him running down the hallway, screaming in Chinese. I realised he was excited! It made me laugh so hard, but I was touched to see what that photo meant to him.

On my last day in Hong Kong I was given a bouquet of flowers, which I passed on to Thomas to give to his mother. He was overwhelmed. He may have worked in a grand hotel, but I knew that every day he went home to a one-bedroom apartment that had six to eight people living in it.

In a lot of the places I visited there was a huge gap between the rich and the poor, which wasn't typical in 1980s New Zealand. It was very hard to witness how some people lived, but one thing that soon became apparent to me was that your happiness is not dependent on how much money you have. The people who had very little financially and were living in poor conditions were often the ones with the biggest smiles on their faces.

Some of the happiest people I saw lived in Latin America. My chaperone Shoshanna tried to prepare me for the reception I would get in those countries.

'Latin American people go crazy for beauty queens, especially Miss Universe,' she told me.

It was all very well to be warned, but the response I got on my first trip to that part of the world still blew me away. As I landed in Colombia, I couldn't believe how big the crowd waiting for me was. They were clapping and cheering as I made my way through the airport. It was a relief to be surrounded by bodyguards because people were yelling and pushing and trying to touch me.

I was driven to my hotel in a white Mercedes surrounded by traffic police on motorcycles, who had their sirens blaring. My

Meeting the locals on my travels.

room was beautiful and had been filled with at least ten bouquets of flowers, and I had my own private maid.

I couldn't help laughing and thinking, *All this for me—Lorraine Downes from Pakuranga!*

My trip to Colombia was on behalf of Catalina, a swimwear company that was one of the biggest sponsors of the Miss Universe competition. My duties included appearing in fashion shows, and at the end of each event, when I came out in my sash and crown, the audience would go absolutely crazy. It felt surreal.

I made several trips to Latin American countries during my year as Miss Universe, and I fell in love with the passion that the people there display. They're not afraid to show their emotions about life, and I admire the way they hold nothing back.

On that first visit to Colombia I had to do quite a few media interviews, and during the last one, the reporters actually clapped when I gave my answers to their questions. The next day, the headline in one of the papers read, 'Wherever Miss Universe Lorraine Downes goes, the world smiles'.

It was moments like those that made me feel it was all worthwhile. The way I was received by many people showed that my presence did make them feel good, and I was very happy about that.

Yes, Miss Universe is all a modern-day fairytale in a way, but hey, if it brings a little joy into somebody's life, then that is a good thing as far as I'm concerned.

On 9 July 1984, exactly 364 days after I had won the Miss Universe title in St Louis, I was in Miami for the final of the next pageant.

'It doesn't seem a year since I said to a lovely young lady from New Zealand, "You are the new Miss Universe,"' declared Bob Barker, introducing me just before the new winner was crowned. 'We all know that the new Miss Universe will find that her title carries even more prestige because it was worn so well by her predecessor.'

I did the traditional farewell walk as the sound system played

Me and Leanne Hosking making a new friend. I look so brave and breezy in this picture, but I'm actually terrified of cats!

a recording of my voice, in which I thanked everyone and wished my successor all the best. I looked very different to the nineteen-year-old who'd been crowned the previous year. Gone was the Lady Di gown, the fluffy hair and flicked-up fringe—I was much more sophisticated in a strapless white gown with my hair pulled back in a sleek style. And I looked so much more confident than I had a year earlier—you could see the change in me.

Miss Sweden, Yvonne Ryding, was announced as the winner, and I couldn't wait to put the crown on her blonde curls. It was such a relief to be Miss Universe no longer—I felt free.

'I looked very different to the nineteen-year-old who'd been crowned the previous year. Gone was the Lady Di gown, the fluffy hair and flicked-up fringe.'

It had been an incredible year that completely changed my life, but it had also been very demanding, and I was ready to go home to my family and friends. I'd had to put Lorraine Downes aside while I concentrated on being this fantasy creation, Miss Universe, and it was time to get on with being me. I wanted to have control over what I did and didn't do.

One of the questions I was frequently asked during my reign as Miss Universe was how it felt to have been crowned the most beautiful woman in the world.

My reply was always, 'I'm not; I don't believe there is such a thing.'

That's not what people wanted to hear but, to my mind, I wasn't the most beautiful of the eighty contestants there on the night of the 1983 pageant in St Louis. I was the person the judges deemed most suitable to do a particular job.

I hope I did it well. I certainly tried my hardest to be as professional as possible.

I was very happy to hand over the Miss Universe title to Yvonne Ryding.

Something else I'm often asked is what was the best thing to come out of that year. There were lots of good things: I grew wiser, I learned a lot about human nature and I got to see many varying aspects of life. I had to grow up pretty quickly.

But for me, one of the highlights was getting to know Ruth Romero. Without her guidance and support, that year would have been a nightmare. I was very naïve, but she helped me to navigate all those new experiences and develop into a more confident young woman.

She also advanced my spiritual awareness, introducing me to books on self-development such as *The Prophet* by Kahlil Gibran and, later, *You Can Heal Your Life* by Louise Hay. Reading about the power of positive and negative thoughts, and the idea that you can choose the way you think—and therefore feel—had an enormous impact on me.

Thanks to Ruth, I learned about being true to yourself. She allowed me to express myself without feeling self-conscious. Her passion for life was contagious and she was fantastic fun; we had a lot of laughs together. I was so lucky that she shared her wisdom with me during that year, and that she has continued to mentor me ever since.

Now in her early eighties, Ruth has aged gracefully and naturally, and is as beautiful now as she was when I first met her—without the aid of any kind of cosmetic enhancement or plastic surgery. She is a living testament that beauty comes from within. When she walks into the room, everyone notices her.

There are thirty years between us, but we are very close friends. I have always called her my *mamacita*—my little mama—and although we may not see one another for years at a time, we keep in touch thanks to Skype. I will forever be grateful to her for being such a wonderful influence in my life.

During that hectic, crazy, unreal year, there were times when I would look at where I was and what I was doing and think, *Why me? Why has this happened to me?*

Today I know that it was my destiny to win the Miss Universe title, and it was for a deeper reason than the experiences I had that year. Being Miss Universe gave me a public profile, which to be honest is not something I have always felt comfortable with; I am still a shy person at heart. But over the years, that profile has given me a voice to create awareness of initiatives I feel very strongly about—including organisations that support cancer patients. It has provided me with opportunities to help people, which I wouldn't have had otherwise, and for that I am very grateful.

I believe it was no fluke that I won. I think it was God's plan for me.

Chapter Six

During my year as Miss Universe, I had counted down the days until I could go home to New Zealand to be with my family and friends. I couldn't wait to head down to Mount Maunganui and hang out at the beach, and I was excited about resuming my modelling career. But there was another reason why I was keen to go home: I had fallen in love.

On a trip to Johannesburg for the Miss South Africa pageant, I was the guest of honour at a cocktail party attended by a few other visitors from New Zealand. One of them was a tall, good-looking guy named Murray Mexted. I had no idea that he was an All Black, although I thought he looked quite sporty.

The next day, Murray sent me flowers and included his phone number on the card. I didn't ring him—I'm not sure why—but he called me and asked if I'd received the flowers.

'Yes, I did—thank you very much,' I said.

'So you weren't going to call me and say thank you? That's rude!'

I apologised, and we started chatting.

'This is my last night in South Africa, and there's a farewell party at a nightclub—maybe we could catch up there,' I suggested.

I gave him the name of the club, and said I might see him later. Unfortunately, the people organising the party didn't realise until the last minute that the club was closed for renovations, and they changed the venue. I had no way of contacting Murray to tell him about the new location—there were no cellphones in those days—so he turned up at the club to find it closed.

He wondered at first if I was giving him the runaround, but then figured that I seemed like a nice girl who wouldn't have done that on purpose. He made a few phone calls and found out where we were, and when he walked in the door, my heart beat a little faster.

He joined our table, and after a while he asked Ruth if she would like to dance. The music had a Spanish feel to it and Ruth was in her element on the dance floor, doing the flamenco around Murray as he got down on one knee and clapped.

One of the party organisers could see that I was desperate to be on the dance floor with Murray, so he asked me up to dance. Shortly afterwards, we swapped partners with Murray and Ruth, and I got to dance with my fellow Kiwi.

Later, Murray admitted that his plan had been to get Ruth on side first, so that he could get closer to me. And it worked!

I couldn't stop thinking about him. In a phone call home not long afterwards, I told Dad my news.

'I've met a guy called Murray Mexted. He plays rugby—have you ever heard of him?'

Dad was so excited. He was a big rugby fan, but none of us girls had ever shown any interest. He would ask if we wanted to get up in the middle of the night to watch international test matches with him, but he always got a no—we thought he was crazy.

Once I returned home I was able to spend more time with Murray, and it soon became clear to me that I'd fallen head over heels in love with him. But I also wanted to further my modelling career, and that meant working overseas. Eileen Ford of Ford Models, one of the biggest and best-known agencies in the world, wanted me to go back to New York to model for Ford, but I needed to build up my portfolio first.

I knew that if I didn't get myself some international work I would grow too comfortable at home and never do it. So I booked a ticket to Sydney, found myself an agency there and flew over.

Modelling jobs in Sydney (top) and Japan (above). Photographers unknown.

Naïvely, I had thought that my stint as Miss Universe would open doors for me, but it didn't. Most people in the modelling world weren't interested in beauty queens—in fact I was told not to mention Miss Universe because it could count against me.

Perhaps I should have expected that response, based on an experience I had in South Africa during my reign. I heard that Johnny Casablancas from Elite Models in New York was staying at my hotel and wanted to meet me, so I went to his room on my way to a Miss Universe cocktail party. But I was out of there about forty-five seconds later. My hot-rollered curls, coral lipstick and sequinned fairy-princess dress obviously did not impress him. He was after someone who could do edgy, high fashion, not a Barbie doll lookalike.

The modelling scene in Australia was really quite aggressive, and I felt like I was having to begin again from scratch. I came home for six weeks over Christmas, then decided to move on to Tokyo, where I was taken on by Ford Models' Japanese branch. My time there didn't get off to a very good start—when I walked in to their office, the assembled staff started pointing at me and talking among themselves in Japanese. They didn't look very happy.

It turned out that the problem was my tan: I was as brown as a berry after six weeks on the beach in New Zealand, and the Japanese like their models to have pale skin. I couldn't work for two weeks while I waited for my tan to fade.

I'd been so eager to try modelling overseas, but I didn't enjoy my time in Japan. After being away from home for so long as Miss Universe, I missed New Zealand. And I missed Murray.

One day I was sitting on the floor at a casting in Tokyo with about 200 other models, waiting for my chance to show my portfolio—it was my tenth 'go-see' of the day—when I was struck by the realisation that I didn't want to do this anymore. I definitely didn't want to travel around the world trying to get work, and I didn't really want to model either. My heart just wasn't in it.

I got on a plane and came home, my modelling career over. But what on earth was I going to do for work?

One of the things that had bowled me over about many of the other contestants in the Miss Universe pageant was how confident they were. They seemed to have so much self-belief and poise; things that I didn't tend to see among Kiwi girls.

I wanted to share what I had learned from being Miss Universe with teenage girls in New Zealand who didn't have that kind of confidence. I came up with the idea of running grooming courses, and got together with Angela Dunn, who'd become a dear friend after our time together in the Julie Cotter Dancers. She had started her modelling career around the same time as I had.

Running the courses was a lot of fun, and helped to fulfil my long-held desire of being a teacher. We focused on personal presentation as a way of ultimately building self-confidence. My philosophy is that having a positive sense of self has to begin with your inner self, so I started the course by asking the participants to write down three things they liked about themselves, and three things they didn't.

Most of the girls found it easy to write down three things they disliked, but often the space for the things they liked was left blank. It was my job to get them to be able to fill in those three things by the end of the course. I loved helping them find what made each of them unique and special, their 'essence'.

On the last day we held a graduation ceremony and invited parents along. Seeing how each girl had blossomed into the best version of herself—someone she was always capable of being, but hadn't realised until she'd been helped in the right direction—nearly always made me cry. It was very sad though when some girls had no family members there to see them graduate: unfortunately there were some parents who were just too busy to be able to attend the thirty-minute ceremony.

In that year after I returned home from my Miss Universe adventures, Murray and I returned to South Africa where we'd met. We took a trip to Victoria Falls, on the border of Zambia and Zimbabwe. It was an incredibly romantic spot, and when he

Me and Angela Dunn
in a promo shot for our
business. I'm not sure what
was going on with our
hairdressers at this time.

Becoming Mrs Lorraine
Mexted, 15 February 1986.

proposed to me there I said yes with no hesitation at all. I was madly in love with him and couldn't wait to be his wife.

We married on 15 February 1986, when I was twenty-one and Murray was thirty-two. The age gap didn't worry me. Looking back, I can see he had a lot more life experience than I did; I entered the relationship not really having a strong identity or a clear idea about what I wanted in life. At the time, I was happy to be guided by him.

By then, Murray had finished playing for the All Blacks and was working for his family's car business in Wellington. I left Auckland and moved down there with him, setting up my own business, an agency called Care of Lorraine Models and Talent. I continued the grooming classes for teenagers and added in night courses for working women, along with corporate grooming seminars.

That side of the business was easy because I'd had experience in Auckland, but setting up a model and talent agency was a challenge. Six years later, when I sold the business, I had around 300 people on my books. But when I started it, I had nobody. I had to go out talent spotting—looking for girls and guys who would make suitable models—and then train them to a high standard.

I was confident that this was something I'd be good at, thanks to my own experiences in the industry. I also knew how to produce fashion shows, and that would eventually become a big part of my business. A lot of local TV programmes were made in Wellington at the time, so there was further work to be had in sourcing people to appear in shows and TV commercials.

I was very excited about the possibilities, but it wasn't easy getting support from people in Wellington. They are loyal to their own there, and I think they assumed my presence in the city was a temporary thing. I held an opening party for the agency and invited all of the important people in the industry, but when only about a third of them turned up, I was really upset. Clearly, I had a lot of hard work to do when it came to establishing business relationships.

My first year in Wellington was spent knocking on people's doors—literally—and asking them to give Care of Lorraine a go.

I was relentless, and slowly people started using the models on my books.

I prided myself on being highly professional in all dealings with my clients, models and talent. For example, I made sure I paid my models as soon as the client paid me—I knew this had been a problem for some models with other agencies.

Once I found my feet I loved running the agency, and I felt that I was doing a good job.

And then everything started unravelling.

I couldn't run the agency on my own, so I'd invited friends from Auckland to come to Wellington to work for me. They were a couple: the wife became my agency manager, and the husband modelled for me. For a few years, things seemed to be going really well, until I heard on the grapevine that the woman was planning on moving to an opposing company. I asked her if this was true. She said no.

However, I found evidence that this was exactly what she was planning and, sure enough, it did happen. What upset me was not so much the fact that she wanted to leave—I'm a big believer in doing what is right for you and moving on if it's what you need—but that she wasn't upfront about it, and that she began the process of going to work with a rival agency while she was with me. We had been really close (or so I thought), and I was very hurt. I just wished she had been able to come to me and share that she wasn't happy in her role.

Her husband—who she'd separated from by then—continued to work for me as a model and also helped me to produce fashion shows. One day he announced that one of my existing clients had asked him to produce a big show for them, and he wanted to use my models.

I was taken aback. Fashion shows were the part of my business I was particularly known for, thanks to my experience and knowledge and the way I'd trained my models. I had an elite group of catwalk models to offer clients, and I didn't understand why this existing client hadn't asked me to do the show.

My gut told me that something was very wrong, so I said to my colleague, 'I am happy for you to do the show, but you will need to find your own models.'

Wellington was too small a market for two people to be producing shows; there wasn't enough work. I didn't think it was right that he should be using the models on my books. However, I knew this decision might cause problems with my models, because

> 'I had an elite group of catwalk models to offer clients, and I didn't understand why this existing client hadn't asked me to do the show. My gut told me that something was very wrong.'

they would be keen to do the show he was organising.

The next day, about six of my top models came to see me and told me they wanted to do the show. I had no choice but to let them go. As each one collected her portfolio and left, I felt very hurt. Some of these girls had never modelled before joining my agency, and I had taught them everything I knew, providing them with lots of work over the years.

I called a meeting and explained the situation to my remaining models. One good thing that came out of the experience was that those who decided to stay made a point of telling me how much they appreciated everything I had done for them. That meant a lot to me.

Later on, I found out my former right-hand man had told some of the models that I wasn't putting them forward for jobs, which simply wasn't true. But that explained why some of them had left—they thought I wasn't looking out for them.

The man went on to set up his own agency using my former models. It closed not long afterwards, but I was still devastated by what had happened. I'd been close to both the man and his wife, and trusted them implicitly. Yes, they had the right to take opportunities that presented themselves and move on in the industry—I had no problem with that. But as is so often the case, it is not what you do but how you do it that is important.

A great example of how to do things properly was shown to me by actor Karl Urban. He's now an internationally famous movie star, having appeared in films like *Star Trek*, *Dredd* and *Thor: Ragnarok*, but when he was starting out in Wellington he was on my books.

There was a role going that he really wanted, but I was unable to get him an audition. He came to see me, and told me that another talent agency could get him the audition, so he would be leaving me to join them.

> 'I believe that in any situation, you must always speak your truth. I respect people who speak the truth and live by it.'

'I'm disappointed to lose you, but you must do what you need to,' I told him. 'Thank you for telling me.'

That was the right way to handle things. Karl was totally upfront with me and I appreciated that. I had to accept that I couldn't do what he needed me to do, and there was a good reason he was moving on.

I believe that in any situation, you must always speak your truth. Yes, it can be painful and hurtful to others, but being dishonest is more hurtful. I respect people who speak the truth and live by it.

In 1992, I decided to sell Care of Lorraine Models and Talent. I'd been doing it for six years and I'd established a great reputation, but it was now time for me to move on. I was thrilled to pass the business on to my very capable agency manager, Bron Eichbaum, and to see the agency flourish thanks to her innate creative talent and her hard work. It continued for many years.

Part of the reason I felt it was time to go was that I was pregnant with my first child. I wanted to be a very hands-on mum, and that can be tricky when you are running a business. Heading a successful agency requires long hours; you have to be available 24/7 for when the big commercial castings come through. I didn't want to be doing that with a baby.

But I had also been deeply hurt by what had happened with the couple who went behind my back, and it was time for my life to change. That experience really shook me, and I learned some hard lessons about trust.

Still, as upsetting as that scenario was, it did not compare to the first true heartbreak I had experienced four years earlier. That was utterly devastating, and left a huge hole in my life.

Chapter Seven

On 25 February 1988—two years after I'd married Murray and moved to Wellington—I was back in Auckland doing promotional work for some of my models.

My agency manager was with me, and we were both staying with my parents in Pakuranga. My beloved *mamacita* Ruth happened to be in Auckland at the same time, and we'd all gone out for dinner with her. During the meal, Dad turned to me and said, 'Lorraine, life is too short to be unhappy.'

At the time I didn't give a lot of thought to what he said but, as it has turned out, that was the most important piece of advice he ever gave me. I think about those words often.

After a lovely evening out, we all headed off to bed. Early the next morning, I was woken by screaming. It was my mother, yelling for me to come quickly. When I got to my parents' bedroom, I found my father had collapsed on the bed. He was having a heart attack.

It was not his first heart attack—he'd had one five years earlier, before I went to Miss Universe. On that occasion, I'd been out on a modelling job when Dad arrived home from work looking pale. He thought he had severe heartburn, so he'd stopped at a shop on the way to buy a packet of antacids. He made it to our house but then collapsed with chest pain, and that night at the hospital we were told that the heart attack had done extensive damage to his heart. There was a chance he might not make it.

Dad was our rock, and none of us could believe he might not pull through. But he did, and he was even well enough to

My beloved dad, Lloyd
William Downes.

travel to St Louis for Miss Universe. His doctors advised him to make some lifestyle changes, including not working so hard. As a plumber he worked long hours, and that had to stop. He and I would go for walks every night, which was not only good for his fitness but also gave us precious time to talk.

There was a history of heart disease in his family, and another heart attack was a possibility. But it was still a huge shock when it happened again in 1988. He got up that morning and told Mum he was going to clean the pool while she had a shower—only for her to come out of the bathroom and find him collapsed on the bed.

I quickly rang an ambulance, but it seemed to take an eternity to arrive. When it did, the staff did not have the right equipment on board to treat a heart attack, even though I had told the 111 operator what was happening to him, so we had to wait for another ambulance. Those paramedics worked on Dad for about an hour but he didn't make it. He was only fifty-four.

After Dad passed, Mum and I sat with him while we waited for my sisters to arrive. He looked so peaceful and beautiful—it seemed as if he was just having a sleep. I'm glad I saw him like that.

Later on, I left the bedroom and was unaware that the funeral directors had arrived. I looked down the hallway and saw the black bag they'd put his body in, which was awful. Worse was yet to come—a few days later we decided to see Dad one last time at the funeral parlour. I wish I hadn't, because they'd put make-up on him, and it dramatically changed the way he looked. I ran out of the room, shocked and upset at what I'd seen.

I didn't want to remember Dad like that, so I decided that I would choose my last memory, and it would be the way he looked as he lay peacefully on the bed at home.

That night I slept with Mum, who was still in deep shock and very upset. At one stage she sat up in bed and said, 'When did we last make love?' She and Dad had been married for thirty-three years; they shared a great love that had not diminished as the years passed, and she had just lost him forever.

We four girls have always been there for her, but it is not the same as having Dad by her side. We were happy for Mum when she met her current partner, Noel, several years after Dad passed.

Me and my sister Sue
on our last dinner out
with Dad.

Noel is very much a part of our family and we know that Mum was lucky to find such a great friend and companion.

It has been nearly thirty years now since Dad died, but for all of us the loss still feels very real. The tears are flowing now as I write this.

About a year after Dad died I went to Bali for the first time, and found it to be an incredibly spiritual place. One day I was having some quiet time, thinking about him.

'Dad, I miss you so much, but I know I have to stop wanting you to still be here with us, and let you go. Please stay close and watch over me,' I said.

I came home from Bali feeling a little more peaceful, and since then I have often felt Dad's presence with me. I know he has seen everything that has happened to me.

I get a lot of comfort from going to see clairvoyants, and whenever I have been to one, Dad has come through. The first time was in Wellington.

'Has your father passed? I have a tall gentleman here with dark, wavy hair and smiling blue eyes who wants to tell you something,' the woman said to me.

Through her, he told me, 'I'm so sorry I never had the chance to say a proper goodbye to you, Lorraine. I really wanted to, so I am saying it now.'

That meant so much to me. When you lose someone you love dearly very suddenly, not having the chance to say goodbye really hurts.

One of the hardest things about losing Dad so early—I was just twenty-three—was that he never got to meet my children. He would have been a wonderful grandfather and, in particular, I wish I could have seen him with my son, Hilton. Dad dearly loved his four daughters, but he would have been thrilled to have a boy.

Murray and I waited until we had been married for five years to start a family and, by the time I got pregnant with Hilton at age twenty-seven, I was very ready to be a mother. I had watched my mum with us girls, and I couldn't wait to have children of my own and be the kind of loving, hands-on mother she was.

As soon as I found out I was pregnant, my life changed. I could feel I was about to embark on a new journey that would involve finding out a lot about myself and what I wanted from life. I was acutely aware that I was bringing someone very precious into the world, who was going to need me for everything, and that was a huge responsibility. It was a time of huge growth for me—not just in the physical sense!

> 'The arrival of a baby is a tough time for many new parents, who have to adjust to having this helpless little person in their lives. It certainly changed the dynamics between Murray and me.'

I loved being pregnant, and could not read enough about all the miraculous changes my body was going through. When Hilton was born on 23 August 1992, I looked down at the innocent child I held in my arms and knew life would never be the same again. This little being needed me, and I was going to be there for him all the way.

The arrival of a baby is a tough time for many new parents, who have to adjust to having this helpless little person in their lives. It certainly changed the dynamics between Murray and me. We'd had a lot of fun together as a couple, but when I got pregnant and my outlook on life began to change, I assumed Murray would change too.

Having Hilton and, five years later, our daughter Jasmine—both of whom were created out of our love—exposed the fact that we wanted to live our lives in different ways. When it became clear that our marriage was in trouble, we began having counselling, together and separately, to try to save it. Those vital

A precious moment
with Hilton.

sessions allowed us to understand one another's differences. I was very young when we got married, and Murray had lived a lot of life. That was one of the things that I was attracted to: the fact that he was so worldly. I thought he knew best, and I can see now that I got lost in his shadow.

I can also see that there were things we didn't really know about one another. We hadn't lived together before we got married, and we'd never discussed what we believed made a marriage and a family work.

Yes, there was a great love between us, and obviously you need to have that, but I have come to realise that the most fundamentally important factor in a successful marriage is compatibility—and we lacked that in some key areas.

Counselling helped me to understand that I wanted Murray to change and be something he wasn't able to be at that stage of his life. It was nobody's fault; it was just the reality we were facing. We needed different things from one another to be happy.

I learned that I needed intimacy in my relationship with my partner, and I don't mean in a sexual way. Having a deeper, spiritual connection with another person was important to me, but Murray didn't need that as much as I did. That was probably the biggest incompatibility between us.

Becoming a mum had helped me to understand myself and find my voice, and I knew I had to speak out. It was time to be honest about who I was and what I needed in my life to be happy.

I did everything in my power to save my marriage, but in the end I had to accept that we couldn't stay together. It takes courage to admit that your relationship has to break up to save yourself, but I just had to do it, as devastating as it was. I never, ever expected to get divorced—as far as I was concerned, marriage was forever. I had seen how strong and loving my parents' marriage was, and that's what I wanted for me and Murray. Unfortunately, it wasn't to be.

I knew we could be wonderful parents to our children, but not together. I wanted Hilton and Jasmine to see us as happy adults, not sad and distant people. That's what we would have been if we had stayed together.

The family photo that Murray and I sent to our loved ones when we decided to separate. We wanted our kids to know that we would always be a family.

Murray and I decided to separate in 1999, and before it became public knowledge, we took a family photo and sent it to our families and closest friends. We explained that we were separating, but that we would always be a family because we were Hilton and Jasmine's parents.

I think couples have a responsibility to work through things as amicably as possible when children are involved. I know sometimes this is very difficult, but it is so important for the sake of the children's wellbeing.

We made it our mission to ensure that our children never felt bad about our separation, or the divorce that followed two years later, and I believe we managed to achieve this. They adjusted very well and I have never seen any sign of them being emotionally scarred by it.

Jasmine was only two when we separated, and she has never really known any different. On her first day of school, the teacher asked the class to draw a picture of their house. Jasmine drew two houses.

When the teacher showed me the picture, the truth that Jasmine came from a broken family really hit me, and I got very upset.

'But this is healthy,' said the teacher. 'Jasmine told me, "This is Mummy's house and this is Daddy's house and I get to have two homes." She's very proud of her two homes—it's fantastic!'

Hilton and Jasmine understand why Murray and I separated, and they know there is no animosity between us. We've had dinners and birthdays together; we've been there for the kids at important occasions. Our families have remained close—I recently had lunch with Murray's sister, and he stayed with my sister Jenny when he came up to Auckland for a rugby match.

Murray has remarried to a lovely woman called Mariska, whom I like and respect very much. They have a beautiful daughter, Hanalei, who is adored by Hilton and Jasmine, her half-brother and -sister. In fact, Hanalei has stayed with us in the past.

Things could have been very different if Mariska wasn't the person that she is, but from the moment she met my children, she has loved them as if they were her own.

Jasmine and I have
always had a close bond.

A while ago I sent an email to Mariska.

'I just wanted to express to you how blessed Murray and I have been to have you in our lives,' I wrote. 'You have made a transition time for our children, and also for Murray and me as co-parents of our children, happen peacefully and with ease. I am very grateful for the woman you are and the love you gave Hilton and Jasmine from day one.'

A reply came back from Mariska.

'Morning, Lorraine. What a lovely way to start my day with a message like that. We all played a part, so it is a team effort really.'

As it turned out, Murray and I were both lucky to find the wonderful people we went on to marry. And as hard as it was when our relationship ended, if it hadn't happened I would never have got the chance to be with the man who was my true soulmate.

Chapter Eight

While there were no bad feelings between Murray and me when our marriage didn't work, there were a lot of sad ones.

I dealt with those feelings by concentrating all my energies on looking after our children. Spending time with Hilton and Jasmine was the perfect antidote to the deep sorrow I was experiencing; being their mother is the best thing I have ever done, and also the thing I think I have done best. I love being a mum.

Although I had a part-time image consultancy business, I was pretty much a stay-at-home mum, and I cherished that. Some women say they could never stay home with their children because it's not stimulating enough for them, but that was never the case for me. In fact it was the opposite: every moment was precious. I believe that the strong bond I have now with Hilton and Jasmine is due to all the time I shared with them from the day they were born. They both know where they sit in my heart.

When it came to parenting, I tended to follow the example set by my wonderful mum. She believes children thrive on routine, and her philosophy certainly seemed to work for my two. They were in bed by 7 p.m. and up again at 6.30 a.m., when they'd come into my bed to start the day with cuddles. I never allowed them to sleep with me, as much as I would have loved it. I knew it would be a habit that would be hard to break later, and I needed my sleep. I'm a light sleeper, so having two wriggling children in the bed was never going to work.

From the word go, I taught Hilton and Jasmine not to be ashamed of sharing their feelings, and to own up to their mistakes. When I did something wrong, I always made sure I said sorry to them. I wanted my kids to know that it's okay to make mistakes, but you must take responsibility for them. I also felt it was important for them to learn about respect—and I believe you can't demand respect from children; you have to earn it.

My children are both loving and respectful, but they have very different personalities. Jasmine is the extrovert. Hilton is bright and cheerful, too, but he has an intuitive side; he's a deep thinker like me.

As a boy, Hilton was a divine little fellow with a beautiful cheeky grin and an incredibly caring nature. I tried not to ever get upset in front of him, but one day when he was about five, I was crying over something and my gorgeous little boy decided to make me laugh. He got a tea towel from the kitchen and wrapped it around my head, like a granny's scarf. It made me feel silly, and of course I laughed.

'See, Mummy, I can make you laugh!' he said, so proud of himself. That's just typical of how kind he is. He used to tell me he loved me so much that he was going to marry me when he grew up.

When it came time for Hilton to start kindy, I enrolled him at a Montessori school; I liked their philosophy of allowing children to decide what they wanted to do with their time. But it didn't suit his personality. I think he needed a more fixed programme, because he chose to spend his time in the sandpit, ignoring the learning activities inside. On his last day, the head teacher described him as a 'challenging young boy', which upset me. Spirited and full of energy, yes, but not challenging.

From there he went to Wadestown Side School. On his first morning I had a good cry in the car after I'd dropped him off—it was so hard to let go!—and I couldn't wait to see him again at the end of the school day.

He ran into my arms and told me what a great day he'd had. On the way out the principal stopped us.

'Hilton is a wonderful boy and we're so happy to have him here,' he said.

That's when I realised the importance of finding the right

While I'm not a rugby fan, I have spent many a winter's day happily watching my son play.

learning environment for your children. Hilton needed more structure, and having that made a world of difference to his learning. Later he went to Wellesley College, a boys' school, and he really thrived there because they understood how boys worked.

Hilton loved rugby from an early age. It had nothing to do with his dad's influence; he just had a natural passion for the game. My Saturday mornings in winter were spent on the sidelines of rugby games, after which I'd stand outside in the cold, hosing the mud off Hilton's rugby gear before it could go anywhere near the washing machine.

In summer Hilton played cricket. He was talented at both, but rugby won out in the end because cricket matches went on too long, taking up too much of his Saturday. He did go on to play rugby overseas, but he's now embarking on a career in hospitality.

As much as I loved and adored my son, I always wanted a daughter, and I felt so blessed to have Jasmine. Hilton, who was five at the time, came up with her name. Heavily pregnant, I was watching the DVD of the animated movie *Aladdin* with him.

'Hills, if this baby is a girl, what should we name her?' I asked.

'Princess Jasmine, after Aladdin's girlfriend,' he said.

I instantly loved the name—although we dropped the princess bit.

From the moment he first saw her, Hilton adored his little sister. Jasmine came into the world smiling, and has stayed that way ever since. She's always had such a happy, cheerful and playful personality, and she never woke up crying like most babies do—mind you, neither did Hilton.

Jasmine was an extremely easy child who did everything I said. I couldn't believe my luck!

As well as being born smiling, Jasmine came out of my womb dancing. When she was just hours old, I noticed her long fingers making graceful movements. Whenever I played music, her body would move to it, so it's no surprise that she has ended up being a dancer.

Jasmine and me at her graduation from Dance World, a top performing arts school in Melbourne.

She started ballet at age five, and later learned jazz and contemporary dance. Jasmine had a true passion for dance and was disciplined right from the start. She went to classes every day except Sunday, and sometimes she would dance on Sundays, too, if there were group practices or competitions held over the weekend. She even changed schools in Year 11 to go to Saint Kentigern College, because it offered dance as an NCEA subject.

As well as the usual classes at her dance school, Mount Eden Ballet Academy (MEBA), Jasmine had extra private lessons, and the only way to fit those in was to go during her lunch hour. Saint Kent's was very supportive and allowed her an extra half hour for lunch on the days when she had a study period straight afterwards.

I'd pick her up and drive her to MEBA while she changed into her ballet gear on the back seat and had a bite to eat. After her class, which required 100 percent concentration, she'd switch clothes in the car again as we headed back to school. It was crazy, but that's how committed she was to dancing. And that's what helped her to win a prestigious scholarship to a top performing arts school in Melbourne when she was only sixteen.

Being with my children helped me survive those difficult dark days after my marriage ended, but there were times when I needed grown-up support. My wonderful family were 600 kilometres away in Auckland, so God sent another mentor and earth angel into my life.

I met Jean Podmore when she came to work for Murray and me as our cleaner. A petite five-foot-two bundle of energy, Jean could make a house shine like no one else. The pleasure she got from her work showed in the end result. She taught me that no matter what you do in life, if you are positive and put love into it you will feel good.

Jean did the cleaning for a lot of people in Wellington, and everyone who employed her knew they were getting so much more than a sparkling home. She had a huge heart, and wherever she went she sprinkled love and wisdom in her own special way.

When Jean finished her work around the house, she and I would sit down for a cup of tea and a chat. From the beginning we just clicked. She was twenty-five years older than me, but that didn't matter; she showed me age is just a number. We soon became close friends, and whenever possible I would try to arrange my schedule so that I was home when she cleaned. I looked forward to her presence: when she was there our house was so much more than super-clean; it was filled with a sense of calm.

Jean would sometimes look after the children when I needed to go away for work, and it was a relief to know they were being cared for so well, in the same way I would care for them. Hilton and Jasmine adored her because she was so loving, and they found her great fun to be around.

Jean didn't drink because she said it didn't agree with her, but she was always the life of the party. Whenever I had friends over for a social gathering, she would be one of the first people to get up and dance with me—I love turning up the music and dancing—and at the end of the evening, she would be the last person to leave. She was always just herself—she never changed the way she was with people, no matter who they were, and I loved that about her.

She had an amazing ability to help people in their times of need. Whether it was sharing advice with young ones, nursing ill people right up to their last days, or offering words of wisdom to couples having relationship problems, Jean would be there and she knew just what to do and say.

I will always be thankful for the help Jean gave me when I was going through tough times. She had a real gift for being able to take away any anxiety I was experiencing. On more than one night before a big corporate grooming presentation, fear would pop into my mind and I would start doubting my ability, but one phone call to Jean would set me right. She knew how to remove my worry and leave me feeling excited about the next day.

'Lorraine, you're successful at what you do—you'll be fine,' she'd remind me.

When my marriage broke up I would be struck by moments of complete grief and fear about the future, which often seemed to occur in the middle of the night. In the light of day things

A treasured photo with my faithful friend Jean Podmore—I have the framed version in my home.

felt manageable, but in the pitch darkness, when everything was so quiet, the stillness seemed to exacerbate my sadness. Those moments could be quite terrifying, but I knew that I could call Jean—regardless of whether it was two or four in the morning—and she wouldn't mind.

'Oh hello, dear,' she'd say. 'Just let me put the kettle on and make a cuppa, and we'll have a chat.'

It didn't matter how long it took, she would find a way to bring me out of that fearful state of mind to the point where I was calm and reassured. I'd be able to hang up the phone and go back to sleep.

Jean was a Christian with a very strong faith in a higher power, and whenever I was facing something difficult she would say to me, 'We'll pray about that, Lorraine.'

One day we had to move a heavy dining table in the apartment building where Murray and I were living at the time. We managed to get it into the tiny old elevator, but when the doors reopened on our floor, we could not for the life of us manoeuvre it out. We were stuck in the lift with the table.

We both got the giggles, which didn't help. Eventually Jean said, 'Lorraine, there's only one way we can get this thing out of here—we need to pray.'

And so she did.

'Dear God, please help us to get this table out of the lift. Come on, God, we really need your help!'

We tried again, and guess what—this time we were able to move the table.

My lovely Jean sadly passed away from cancer in 2012. I miss her dearly, especially when I am struggling with something in my life and I wish I could pick up the phone to hear her calming voice.

But I do know that Jean is always close by, watching over me. One day, when I was really missing her, I said a prayer and asked her to give me a sign that her spirit was with me.

Next thing, I heard the wind banging an outside door, so I went to close it. As I made my way down the side of the house, there lying in the garden was my copy of the order of service from Jean's funeral. It had been sitting on my kitchen windowsill and must have been blown out of the window at some stage.

I sat down in the garden and cried. That to me was proof that my absolute belief in the afterlife was justified.

I will be forever grateful to Jean for sharing her love, and for teaching me about what's important in life.

Faith has always been an essential part of my life. Since I was a child, I've felt that there is something bigger than us at work. And as a young girl, I was always questioning: *Why am I here? What is my purpose?*

My family was brought up in the Presbyterian faith, and on the weekends I went to Sunday school. I loved the messages we were given and I always felt very safe there. As a teenager, a group of my friends were heavily into the Baptist religion and I used to go to church with them. Some had found God, and I wanted to find God too. Part of the church services were very much about speaking in tongues, and sometimes I would sit there, unable to connect with what was going on. For me, God wasn't there.

I would read the Bible, and I loved a lot of what I read, especially the proverbs and psalms. There were messages there that I really wanted to live my life by. But other things did not always resonate with me.

The Bible talks about the power of prayer, and I began praying to my God. And after a while, I started hearing God replying to me.

One of my very first modelling jobs was for a French chewing gum company, as I mentioned earlier. I was in a van with a group of models, en route to the shoot in Northland, when a joint was lit and passed around. I freaked out because I had never smoked marijuana before, but I was worried about saying no because I wanted the other models to accept me. I didn't know how to handle the situation, and I found myself praying.

'Dear God, what do I do? Please help me.'

As clear as anything, I heard a voice say, 'Relax, everything is going to be okay. Just take the joint and pass it on.'

People might think I'm crazy, but that's what I heard. I did what the voice said, and nobody hassled me about not smoking the joint. Since then, whenever I pray, I hear a message in response.

In the past, I tended not to talk about my faith with most people because it's very personal to me, and I didn't want to have to justify it to others. But now I've got to the stage where it doesn't matter what other people think; it is a part of who I am and I couldn't imagine my life without it. My faith—the thing I call God—makes everything so much easier.

'In the past, I tended not to talk about my faith with most people because it's very personal to me, and I didn't want to have to justify it to others. But now I've got to the stage where it doesn't matter what other people think.'

I don't really know how to define my God. The one thing I don't believe is that he's an entity sitting up in the clouds. To me, God is a higher power, an energy that is all around us. This power is bigger than us, but also within us. And to me, it doesn't matter if you're Christian or Buddhist or anything else—I believe all faiths are just the same, with fundamental beliefs that are really similar.

I see God in nature, and in people. Most importantly, I think God is love. I believe that our purpose in life, the reason we are here, is to love and to become enlightened. We're here to learn, and to do that we have to experience both blessings and suffering in our lives. I also believe that life is eternal, and that the people we've lost are around us all the time.

In my day-to-day life, I thank God all the time, and I ask for guidance. I know I can always find comfort in my faith when things aren't going right.

After my marriage broke up, I had another experience that

proved to me that God is always there for us. One night, in the darkness, my pain became overwhelming. I was mourning the loss of my marriage and the break-up of my family, and I ended up on the ground, sobbing.

'God, how am I going to get through this?' I asked in prayer. 'Help me, please!'

And then all of a sudden, it felt as if I were being held in someone's arms. There was a presence, and it was wrapped around me, holding me while I wept.

I stopped crying and felt a calmness wash over me. I was being shown that someone was there with me, and I was loved. It was an incredible experience, and I'll never forget it.

My faith has grown with the passage of time, and today I feel it is stronger than ever. Which is fortunate, because over the past few years I have really needed it.

Chapter Nine

A couple of years after my marriage ended, my dear school friend Patricia came down from Auckland to stay with me for the weekend. We had a lovely time together and, as she left, Patricia handed me a note.

'Lorraine, it's time,' she said.

Patricia wrote in the note that she'd felt my sadness over the weekend, and she thought it was time for me to stop grieving for my marriage and move on.

'You need to be happy again, Lorraine,' she wrote.

I read her kind, loving words, and I knew what she'd said was the truth. I chose, right in that moment, to find joy in life again.

I believe you do have to make a choice to leave behind pain and suffering. Thanks to my beautiful friend, I was able to do that. Patricia has a knack for showing up when I need guidance, and this guidance comes on a spiritual level—it's as if she can see right into my heart and understand exactly what I need. This is why I trust everything she suggests for me. We have a strong spiritual bond, and I am very grateful for my beautiful Scottish friend.

Patricia helped me to see that I needed to rediscover myself. I had been immersed in being a wife, mother and business owner, and I'd stopped pursuing my own interests. This is something that often happens to mothers—we are so busy giving to others that we forget about ourselves.

I thought about what I had enjoyed before marriage and family life, and the thing that immediately came to mind was dancing.

So I decided to take a six-week salsa dancing course. I loved every minute of it! Salsa is such a happy dance—you can't help smiling the whole time you're doing it—and I came home from each lesson feeling uplifted and energised.

In our last session, the instructors asked the class if we would like to see them dance the Argentinian tango. I was mesmerised as I watched them moving to the beautiful music; it was so lovely that it moved me to tears. I knew in that moment that I just had to learn the tango—that's when my long-standing love affair with this stunning dance started.

I began going to milongas (tango events) on Sunday nights, and that brought a lot of joy into my life. I was finally moving on.

I might have been picking up the pieces of my life again, but that didn't mean I was looking for a new relationship—dating was the last thing on my mind. Then, in 2001, I got a phone call from cricketer Martin Crowe.

Marty and I had first met eleven years earlier, when we were hired to present an in-house video for National Bank staff about their corporate images. Despite having zero interest in cricket, I *did* know who Marty was, although I perhaps didn't appreciate that he was regarded as one of New Zealand's best-ever cricketers. All I knew was that he was the captain of the national team.

We worked on the video together for three days, and it's hilarious to watch now. Marty would be instructing male staff how to knot their ties, then he'd go, 'Over to you, Lorraine.'

I'd step in to advise female staff on what pantyhose to wear, before saying, 'Back to you, Martin.' Talk about cheesy.

There was a fair bit of standing around waiting during the shoot, so we chatted a lot, and I found Marty very easy to talk to. He was extremely charming, with a wonderful voice, and was pretty easy on the eye too. He had a lovely energy about him and I enjoyed his company.

During one lunch break he said to me, 'Do you want to get out of here?'

I did, so he took me to a nearby art gallery. That was something

The Argentinian tango
has become one of
my passions.

new to me, but Marty clearly had an interest in paintings. It was a pleasure wandering around, looking at the art with him.

There was definite chemistry between us, but I was married at the time so there was never anything more to it. I never looked at him like *that*.

Not long after we made the video, Marty moved to Wellington and invited me to his housewarming party. I took Murray with me, of course—I had no romantic interest in Marty at all; I just thought he was a nice man.

The next time we spoke was when Marty rang me out of the blue one day, sounding cheeky. He was in the West Indies playing cricket; it was midnight his time and he'd obviously had a few wines.

'Lorraine, I just had to ring you and ask you a question,' he said. 'Are you happily married?'

'Yes, I am,' I told him, which was the truth.

'Okay,' he said. 'I just had to ask.'

Marty later married model Simone Curtice, but the relationship ended in 1996. Fast-forward to 2001, and our paths crossed again. I had a part-time job as a 'fit' model for fashion label Ashley Fogel, and it turned out that Ashley and his wife Wende were friends of Marty's. He was living back in Auckland by then, but he caught up with the Fogels on a visit to Wellington, and they mentioned to him that I was no longer married.

So Marty picked up the phone and rang me. When he asked if I'd like to meet, I said yes. We'd got on well; it would be nice to catch up.

We arranged to see one another at the Massey Memorial in Miramar. It was his birthday, and I thought it would be a good idea to take along a half bottle of Pol Roger champagne. As I pulled it out of my backpack, Marty reached into his bag and drew out a half bottle of Pol Roger, exactly the same as mine. Snap! How incredible was that?

The outing went well, so we decided to go to the movies the following night to see *Captain Corelli's Mandolin*. Unfortunately, that date was not a success. People noticed us together and were pointing and whispering, and I couldn't handle it. I hadn't been out on a date with anyone since separating from Murray, let alone someone so well known, and I felt uncomfortable and uptight. It was impossible to relax.

A couple of other things that happened on the night made me think that maybe this wasn't the best idea after all. I could see that Marty had some issues he needed to sort out.

Afterwards, he rang me all excited about going on another date, and I had to tell him no.

'I'm not ready for this,' I said. 'And I don't think you are either. I think you've got some growing to do.'

He was devastated, but I felt it was the best thing to do. My gut feeling was that there was still 'inner work' to be done by both of us, and I've always been one to listen to my instincts. I think it means a higher power is telling you something is not right, and if you're feeling uneasy about something, it is for a reason.

I didn't go on any other dates after that unsuccessful trip to the movies with Marty. I just didn't feel ready to be in a relationship.

Four years after that night, in 2005, a friend of Hilton's who did feng shui came to our house, keen to offer some advice according to the principles of this ancient art.

'Would you like to meet someone?' she asked me.

'Yes, I would,' I admitted. It had been six years since my split from Murray, and I was starting to feel that maybe the time was right.

'Well, you're going to have to change some things in your home,' she announced.

She walked into my living room, where I had a couch and a single chair.

'Where do you sit?' she asked.

'In the chair.'

'You need to start sitting on the couch, so there's room for someone to sit next to you,' she instructed.

In my bedroom, I had one bedside table and one reading light.

'You've got to start thinking in pairs,' she said. 'You need another table and light.'

She also suggested that I get a picture of two birds and hang it up on the wall. I did everything she said—including opening my mind to the possibility of having a partner again. My mind had been focused on just me and the kids, she said, and I needed to allow somebody else in.

Okay then, I thought. I would do as she recommended. I certainly had nothing to lose.

Two weeks after the feng shui makeover, I was invited to attend a New Zealand Cup Week racing event in Christchurch with fashion designer Petrena Miller. I had been working for her label Petrena for several years, doing two shoots a year for her advertising campaigns and look books. They were long days but lots of fun, and Petrena would let me choose the team we worked with, including my favourite photographer, Monty Adams. Petrena's a total professional, and she understands the importance of getting the right mix of energy on a shoot, so that you get a great end result.

Petrena had become a good friend, and I was happy to go to the races with her and wear one of her beautiful outfits. She wanted to set me up on a blind date while we were there. *Why not?* I thought.

My date was a lovely gentleman, but I knew instantly that he was not for me. We had a good time anyway, and I was enjoying the races, when Petrena casually mentioned that earlier in the day she'd bumped into somebody she knew at Clearwater Resort, where we were staying.

'Martin Crowe is staying in the room next to ours, and he's invited me and my group along for drinks this evening,' she said.

There was a twinkle in her eye as she added, 'Did you know that he is single?'

I didn't. I found out that after our disastrous date, Marty had begun a relationship with a woman named Suzanne Taylor (she later changed her name to Huhaana). They'd had a baby together, a little girl called Emma, but had separated when Emma was two.

There were butterflies in my stomach when I thought about

A selection of my modelling shots for Petrena Miller's fashion label in the mid-2000s.

seeing Marty again. How serendipitous was it that he was in the hotel room next to ours, and that Petrena had run into him?

When Marty opened the door to his hotel room, he got a shock to see that I was part of Petrena's group. But from that moment on, it felt as if the timing was finally right for us. It actually felt like magic—although the situation was challenging for me because my blind date was there too, and I felt I should spend time chatting to them both.

As I spoke to Marty, it became obvious that he had changed in the four years since I had last seen him. Becoming a father had made him a lot more grounded, and less selfish. I liked that.

Marty told me that my decision not to see him again after our date had taken quite an emotional toll, and I apologised for that. It seemed that, this time, both of us were ready to try again.

We talked about going to the movies some time, and then I left and went back to my room next door. Marty, who was a huge music fan, put the James Blunt song 'You're Beautiful' on repeat, and played it over and over, knowing I could hear it through the wall!

The next day Marty had an early golf game, and I didn't see him before I flew home to Wellington. It was a couple of days before he rang me. I was sitting on my bed, and we talked for ages.

'I'm going to come down to Wellington and take you out for lunch,' he told me.

'Okay,' I replied.

When we ended the call, I was like an excited teenager. I started beating my hands on the bed, squealing, 'Yes, yes, YES!'

I instinctively knew that this was the start of something very special.

Marty had noticed how uncomfortable I'd been on our previous date when we were spotted by members of the public, so he booked a private room at a Japanese restaurant for our lunch date. He brought along his iPod and played his favourite music. We sat on the floor and talked, and talked, and talked—it was just so easy to open up to him. I told him my life story and he told me his, and it was so liberating to be myself with him. I felt that I was able to say anything.

Our lunch date ended up lasting five hours; neither one of us wanted it to end. Unfortunately, Marty had to fly back to Auckland for his job as a sports producer for Sky Television. We managed to meet up a couple more times, and then he planned a weekend away for us at Omaha beach, about an hour's drive north of Auckland. Marty's close friend and PA, China Gillman (who I also happened to know—more serendipity!), was very good friends with a man who owned a stunning home there, and China arranged for us to stay with her in the beachside house.

I flew up to Auckland Airport, where Marty was waiting for me, holding a sign that read, 'Rainbow Tours'. During our conversation at the Japanese restaurant, I had told him that my first-ever nickname was Rainbow, and that it had been given to me when I was five by my first love interest. He'd obviously been paying attention!

As we drove up to Omaha, our conversation was once again easy and relaxed. Right from the beginning, I felt that I could just be me—silly me, mad me, quiet me, fearful me, thoughtful me, whatever me. Marty allowed me to simply be who I was, and that was an incredible gift.

We had a fabulous weekend staying in China's friend's home. Before the trip, Marty had asked me what my favourite DVDs were, and he'd tracked all of them down so we had a choice of what to watch. He also brought along a DVD of a New Zealand film called *Rain*, which is my other nickname. From the start, he called me Raine. I called him 'my beautiful man'.

Marty suggested we make a new playlist on his iPod of our favourite music, and it turned out we had the same taste. The more I learned about this man, the more I realised we were in step with one another.

We had separate rooms, and on the first morning he came in to my room very early and woke me up.

'I'm still sleeping!' I told him, and went back to my slumber. When I woke up later, he'd slipped a note under my door, apologising for disturbing me.

Marty and I knew we were onto something special when we reconnected in 2005, and our relationship only grew stronger with time.

He also wrote, 'I'm incredibly grateful that I can share a whole day, any day, with you. It does feel very surreal to be here, so close in your company. I'm overjoyed to be honest. Another moment, another day to connect, is priceless.'

He added, 'The day is going to be stunning and magical in its natural beauty. Just like you.'

I learned then and there that Marty had a way with words, and that he was incredibly romantic.

> 'I learned then and there that Marty had a way with words, and that he was incredibly romantic. As the weekend progressed, our conversations got deeper and we shared the things that were important to each of us.'

As the weekend progressed, our conversations got deeper and we shared the things that were important to each of us. I told Marty that I was on a spiritual path of learning more about my existence and my purpose here on earth. He spoke about a healing session he had experienced in Australia, and how he knew he needed to do a lot of work on himself.

Marty had spent much of his life living with fear—fear of failing, of rejection, of being humiliated. He was just nineteen when he made the New Zealand cricket team and he was put under a lot of pressure, not only by others but also by himself. He could be very self-critical and unforgiving. As he himself put it: a champion at holding on to resentment and bearing grudges. He'd already started facing up to some of his demons; now he was ready to make further changes.

I gave Marty a book called *The Invitation* by the Canadian writer Oriah. It explores how to follow our heart's longing for a life in which we can choose joy, without denying the difficulties we face. It is an incredible work—a map for the soul and for our desire to live passionately, both within ourselves and in our connections with the world around us.

'I love what Oriah has shared in her book,' I told him as I handed him the copy. 'This is where I am at in my life, and I want to grow and learn to live like this.'

He started reading it immediately, and became determined to explore his inner wellbeing and to search for spiritual enlightenment.

It was clear to us both that the timing was right for a relationship. When I got home to Wellington, Marty emailed me something he'd written while we were at Omaha. The strength and beauty of his words was breathtaking.

'These last two days have been beyond belief. Seriously, it has taken my breath away. Right from the start, there has been a succession of moment after moment. We have moved serenely from one to another and have made the most of each one. Added to this is that, for me, the emotional intensity has increased almost every hour.

'Right now, as I look at you by the pool, I feel breathless. My heart is spilling over. I have feelings of genuine love for you. From here, what will be, will be. I have dreams and that is all. My heart is with you and that will not change. I'm happy to risk looking like a fool for you. I want to love well too.

'In the meantime, until we see each other again, I will thrive on my own. As Oriah says, "Because I have to."'

His words blew me away. After several false starts, and a very short amount of time together, Marty and I were deeply in love, on a level that connected our hearts and souls.

I had met my match, and there was no going back.

Chapter Ten

With Marty living in Auckland and me in Wellington, we could hardly go charging headlong into our new relationship. And as parents of children who were still quite young, we were conscious of how they would feel about us being together, and wanted to handle everything sensitively. So we took things very carefully.

I wondered what would happen when the public learned we were a couple. I could see that people might think, *Oh, that Lorraine Downes, she obviously has a thing about sportsmen.* But it was a complete fluke that after being married to an ex-All Black, I ended up with a former Black Cap. As it happens, I don't like rugby, and I don't like cricket, and I've never watched either sport! I fell in love with a person, not the fact that he'd played sport for New Zealand.

I knew there would be public interest. To be honest, I'd quite liked being out of the spotlight since my marriage to Murray had ended, so I wasn't particularly looking forward to it.

But then I went and did something that thrust me back into the public eye. I agreed to take part in *Dancing with the Stars.*

When the first series of *Dancing with the Stars* screened in New Zealand I'd tuned in every week to watch. I loved the show, not just because of the dancing but also because it raised some serious cash for the dancers' chosen charities. But when I was approached and asked if I would be one of the celebrity dancers in the second series, I had to think long and hard about it. It would mean six weeks of practising before the first episode even screened, and then up to eight weeks of learning new dances and performing them live every Sunday—depending on how long I lasted in the competition, of course. Potentially, it could be a three-month-plus commitment. I'm the type of person who gives 150 percent when I agree to do something, and I knew it would be a huge undertaking.

I was concerned about having to spend a lot of time away from my children and I didn't want Hilton, who was thirteen and in his first year at secondary school, to get hassled because his mum was on a TV show. It wasn't the sort of thing that would go unnoticed—it was one of the most-viewed programmes on TV at the time. An average of 730,000 people tuned in every week during the first season, and the final drew around a million viewers.

I asked Hilton if he was okay with me taking part.

'Mum, you should do it,' he replied instantly. 'You get to raise lots of money for charity. Go on!'

Jasmine, who was well into her dancing at the age of eight, was similarly enthusiastic and told me to go ahead.

So that was the children on board; Marty was also supportive. Next, I had to conquer my fear of performing on live TV. If anything went wrong, I couldn't do a retake. I was very nervous about that.

I knew that a lot would hinge on which of the professional dancers was assigned to be my partner. It had to be somebody I liked and trusted completely, and we needed to have a connection—we were going to be spending a lot of time together.

Before agreeing to do the show, I asked the producer Debra Kelleher if I could meet the partner that had been chosen for me. This wasn't usually done, but she agreed, and Aaron Gilmore was flown down from Auckland.

The first thing I noticed when Aaron walked into the café was his beaming smile and the way he looked me straight in the eye when we shook hands. His energy felt very positive. Debra left us to chat, and Aaron filled me in on his dancing experience. He showed me photos of his stunning wife Jaimee and their gorgeous children Ethan and Grace, which I thought was endearing. Aaron was funny, down to earth, genuinely nice and not too hard on the eye, and I knew I would be happy dancing with him.

When Debra returned we had a private conversation.

'Yes, he's perfect!' I told her.

So that was it, then. I had the ideal partner and the support of my kids. I was really going to be on *Dancing with the Stars*.

> 'As well as the strenuous training, the other thing I had to get used to was having a cameraman there filming us constantly . . . Richard was our cameraman, and he witnessed everything we did—and I do mean everything.'

Rehearsals started at the end of March 2006. While I had done salsa and tango before, I had never tried ballroom dancing in my life and there were many dances I had to learn from scratch. People think it must have been easy for me but, believe me, it wasn't.

Things didn't get off to a great start—I had been sent two pairs of gold satin ballroom shoes, and silly me hadn't thought to wear them in first. So fifteen minutes into my first rehearsal with Aaron, while learning the cha cha, I already had blisters on both feet. I also needed to sit down for a breather because I was so unfit. At forty-two, the only exercise I had been doing was the occasional walk, and I was very out of shape.

As well as the strenuous training, the other thing I had to get used to was having a cameraman there filming us constantly. The footage he took would be used in a clip showing what we'd been up to each week, and would be played on the programme just before we danced. We had no idea what was going to be used in the minute-and-a-half package.

Richard was our cameraman, and he witnessed everything we did—and I do mean everything. From emitting natural body sounds (that wasn't me) to accidentally whacking your partner in sensitive parts of their anatomy (I admit to that), he saw it all. The most embarrassing one for me was trying to tell Aaron that I couldn't dance because I had a painful bladder infection.

Aaron and I wanted to choose a word that we could repeat as a kind of affirmation for the whole experience, and the word we came up with was *joy*. There was plenty of joy in what we were doing, even though it was hard work. It was the perfect word to recite, especially when the nerves started to kick in.

The show started off with eight pairs of dancers—each pair made up of a celebrity contestant and a professional partner—and every week one couple was voted off until there were two couples remaining. Apart from the final show, which was decided by public vote, the scoring was shared fifty-fifty between the panel of judges and the public. Proceeds from the public's telephone vote went to each contestant's chosen charity. Because of Dad's heart attack I initially wanted to support the Heart Foundation, but they had already been chosen by discus champion Beatrice Faumuina, so I opted for the Child Cancer Foundation (CCF) instead. I went with CCF because they received no government funding and relied heavily on public donations, and because I knew a couple whose child had cancer and I'd seen how hard it was for the whole family. Little did I know the impact that cancer would have on my own family in the future.

For me, one of the most exciting parts of being involved in *Dancing with the Stars* was the costumes. Before the show started I met with Claire Palmer, the head of the costume department, to discuss the colours I would wear—a matter that was close to my heart because of my work as an image and colour consultant. Claire totally got what I was saying and did an incredible job.

She and her team spent countless hours making our beautiful costumes, often sewing right up until a few hours before the show went live on Sunday night. Every sequin had to be glued on by hand, and there were a lot of sequins!

I was thrilled with every costume made for me. For the first week's dance I was due to wear a red sequinned cha cha dress. I asked for a hemline just below my knee as that was the length I felt most comfortable with. Aaron laughed when he saw it.

'These costumes are just going to get skimpier, Miss Downes; trust me!'

When it came to the last show, he reminded me of what he'd said—my freestyle costume only just covered my bum! Fortunately, all the ladies wore skin-coloured fishnet pantyhose, which helped us feel a little more covered.

The music was a big part of the competition. As soon as we got the text message at the start of each week telling us what our dances were, we would drop everything and scour the list of available music, hoping to beat the others to the song we wanted to dance to. Aaron would then start work on the choreography.

When it came to performance time, we had a live orchestra, led by the wonderful Carl Doy. The live music was fantastic but it often sounded different to the recording we'd been rehearsing to all week, so that took a bit of getting used to.

There were a lot of challenges thrown at us throughout the competition, but we found a way to deal with each one as it arose.

I spent an awful lot of time going to the toilet before our first live performance on 7 May. Aaron and I were the last to perform out of the eight couples, and by the time we went on my nerves were well and truly screaming at me.

Thankfully, all the effort we'd put in over the previous six weeks meant that I pretty much knew what I was doing. We got through the cha cha without anything too dramatic happening, and we didn't get voted off. So the next week we were back to do the quickstep.

It's a wonderful dance, the quickstep—big and sweeping with

Top The beach has always been my happy place. Here I am as a baby with Mum and my sisters Sue (left) and Jenny. Carolyn was still to come.

Above I was a shy child, but grew more at ease in front of the camera in time.

OK

Opposite and above
A couple of my early modelling shots. Years of summer holidays at Mount Maunganui meant that I felt comfortable on the beach in swimwear.

Top Getting to know the other girls was one of the best things about my Miss Universe experience. My roommate Leanne Hosking (Miss South Africa) is seated on my left here.

Left Claiming the Miss Universe throne felt surreal. I couldn't believe I had won.

Opposite My first-ever press conference was conducted over breakfast in bed!

MISS UNIVERSE

Top As Miss Universe, I had to adapt quickly to a life of media interviews and appearances. Although I often felt like a fish out of water, I was determined to represent New Zealand well.

Above My 'Latin American' look, which involved a lot more make-up than I was used to! A make-up artist would travel with me when I visited those countries.

Top A favourite photo with Miss South Africa, Leanne Hosking, and my chaperone and close friend Ruth Romero.

Above The reception I got from the locals in many countries I visited made me feel it was all worthwhile.

A shot from the couple of months I spent modelling in Sydney; photographer unknown. The modelling scene there was tough, and it seemed my Miss Universe win was more of a hindrance than a help.

fast footwork. The problem is that if you get just slightly out of time with your partner, it feels like you're in a washing machine together. I had invited my mum and sisters down for the live show, which was filmed at the Avalon Studios in Lower Hutt. With them watching, I was even more nervous than the previous week. But we made it through, and returned the following week to do the jive.

You would think that by week three I'd have got my nerves under control, but they were worse than ever. I knew that I had to do something about the state I was getting myself into, as it was spoiling my enjoyment of the dancing. I had to have a major talk to myself before the third show.

Just before we went on, I said a prayer.

'Please, God, give me the strength not to let these nerves get the better of me, so I can deliver what I have worked really hard on all week. Thank you.'

I ended with a resounding, 'F*** off, nerves!'

And it worked. I had fun doing the jive and our performance was well received by the judges. We were voted back again for the fourth week.

My nerves started to ease after that, but I still had butterflies before each performance. I'd be jiggling up and down as I stood in the wings with Aaron, listening to our video clip playing (which we couldn't see) and waiting to go on.

Then we'd get the call: 'Would Aaron and Lorraine please take the dance floor.'

The words going through my brain every time were, 'Holy shit, here we go!'

I could sense the anticipation of the judges as we made our way down the stairs to our starting positions. After we finished, I would listen intently to what the judges told us, and so would Aaron. They were true professionals, and I took on board everything they said.

I felt that I was improving, but there were still times when things didn't go quite right. In show four's foxtrot, my beautiful pink floaty sleeves got draped all over Aaron's face as we executed

My wardrobe malfunction during show four's foxtrot. All *DWTS* photos by Neil Mackenzie.

a lift. It was hard not to burst out laughing during what was supposed to be a very romantic dance.

The following week we had the samba. Given my fondness for Latin dance, I was very excited about this one. We danced to Barry Manilow's 'Copacabana' (they changed the name Lola in the lyrics to Lorraine!), and as the track progressed, I could feel myself really getting into it. Then I did a sharp turn to face Aaron—and had a complete mental blank about what to do next! The show's photographer, Neil Mackenzie, captured the moment perfectly: the look on my face in his pictures was pure 'What on earth am I supposed to be doing?'

But that special connection Aaron and I had kicked in, and we somehow kept going and picked up our routine again. I didn't fool judge Brendan Cole though. In his weekly column on the show he wrote, '[Aaron and Lorraine's] was the best samba of the night, despite Lorraine sometimes lacking the confidence to convince us she knew what she was doing.'

He went on to say, 'One advantage this couple seem to have is a chemistry together—that cannot be taught or faked. For some reason it just works and that together with their choreography and abilities shows them settling in as the ones to watch every Sunday.'

For that fifth show we also had to learn a group dance, a Viennese waltz, and I had a lot of fun doing it. I relished being part of a team, something I hadn't always had in my working life. The people on the show were a pleasure to work with, from the crew and production people through to host Jason Gunn, who was not only extremely funny but also very kind and supportive of us all.

The eliminations every week were hard. Even if Aaron and I had danced well we would worry about being voted off, because we didn't do much campaigning to try to win the public over. The amount of time spent rehearsing was up to each couple, and Aaron and I decided to devote as many hours as possible to dancing, leaving little for campaigning. Plus I had two children who needed their mum at home, so there was no opportunity out of hours to do it.

The moment my mind
went blank in the middle
of performing the samba.
My face says it all!

We were well aware that we could go at any time, and it was a huge relief every time we heard our names called out, announcing that we were through to the next round.

It was not easy to see other couples leaving. I was especially sad when *Shortland Street* actress Angela Bloomfield and her partner, Jonny Williams, were voted off. Angela was the mum of a toddler and a baby, and I admired her gutsy efforts in having a young family while taking part in a gruelling TV show.

In week six we had to tackle two dances: the waltz and the rumba. For the waltz I chose Nat King Cole's rendition of 'Unforgettable' and dedicated it to my dad. The goal with all the dances was to tell a story. When it came to the rumba, the dance of love, the aim was to make everyone watching think we were deeply in love. So we needed to draw on another talent—acting! I'm glad we didn't have to do that in the first week. We must have been pretty convincing; we scored a 10 for our rumba.

My costume was a rather revealing red dress, and it had quite a profound effect on Marty, who had come down to Wellington to watch us filming. He used to watch from a set of bleachers that weren't visible on TV, so that he wouldn't be seen by anyone viewing the show. Aaron reckons that when I walked past Marty in the rumba costume, Marty 'went into school-boy mode and blushed'. He wanted to know if I could take the costume home!

Our dances the following week were the tango and the paso doble. I thought that the Argentinian tango classes I'd been to might be useful, but the ballroom version was completely different. In Argentinian tango you keep your partner close in a tight embrace, but in the ballroom dance, you hold your body out and away from your partner and use very sharp head movements—those can give you whiplash if you're not careful. I didn't like it at all.

The paso doble, on the other hand, was a joy. It's a very passionate and dramatic dance in which the man portrays a bullfighter and the woman represents his cape. When we danced the paso doble, it felt for the first time that we were a couple, rather than a professional dancer and a so-called celebrity. And that dance took us through to the next show—which was the final.

We were up against Beatrice Faumuina and Brian Jones, and we knew the standard would be very high. We had to do three dances: two of our previous ones (we chose the waltz and the paso doble) and a freestyle. That meant a lot of work.

On the Wednesday before Sunday's final, I noticed that Aaron wasn't looking great.

'Are you okay?' I asked him. 'You look awful.'

He said he was seeing stars and the room was spinning. Richard, our cameraman, freaked out and called TVNZ. Aaron was sent to the doctor, who advised him to rest.

Aaron knew that the enforced rest would stuff up our schedule, but I told him to take a day off and get better. He slept for seventeen hours straight—a day's worth of rehearsals—but c'est la vie. He needed it.

That week I also had a funeral to go to: my lovely friend Jean's daughter Carol. She was the same age as me; we'd been pregnant together and joined the same antenatal group, and she was a wonderful person. The mother of three beautiful children, Carol had been diagnosed with brain tumours two years earlier, and by the time *Dancing with the Stars* started she was very ill. Carol had been my inspiration throughout the competition, and when she died it was very upsetting. Her death was a reminder about what is truly important: our health and our loved ones.

Going into the final against Beatrice and Brian, Aaron and I decided that we would just focus on having a blast. We had consistently brought our best every week, and felt that we couldn't do any more.

The waltz went smoothly and I felt beautiful out on the dance floor with my amazing partner, who had done so much to help me move like a professional.

But Aaron had something in store for me when it came to the paso doble. When we'd danced it previously, our routine ended with Aaron turning me in three circles and releasing me so that I slid, sitting up, across the floor. But this time, he spun me

Dancing the waltz in the
final show felt magical.

The dramatic finale to
our paso doble on that
last night.

around five times instead of three. By the time I hit the floor I was screaming across it at great pace, and there was no way I could sit upright—I was going to end up flat on my back! I did my best to make the mistake look like part of the plan, flinging out an arm and leg to end the routine with some drama.

Aaron ran over to pick me up as soon as the music stopped, and we were both in hysterics. That's what live television is all about—those human elements.

'By the time I hit the floor I was screaming across it at great pace, and there was no way I could sit upright—I was going to end up flat on my back!'

Luckily our freestyle dance went without a hitch.

When it came time to announce the winner, I was philosophical. *Well, we've tried our hardest, that's all we can do.* Aaron had said right from the beginning that he thought we could win, but he knew it was likely to be close, and it was. The winning couple was decided entirely on public voting, and when our names were read out we shared a moment of pure happiness. It was a huge achievement for me, and I was beyond delighted.

What made winning *Dancing with the Stars* so special was that I got to do it with Aaron. Afterwards, I gave him the trophy to keep because I felt he deserved it far more than me. I would never have won if it wasn't for Aaron. He was the consummate professional throughout; a talented dancer, and a generous one, too. He never tried to out-dance me: he always made sure I shone in the dance, not him. In a show like this, that's what a true professional should do for their celebrity partner.

Aaron was an exceptional teacher. There must have been times when he was frustrated with me because my body and brain wouldn't co-ordinate and I couldn't remember what I had been taught. He never lost it with me once. He obviously sensed that

Top Waiting alongside Beatrice and Brian to hear the outcome of the final public vote.

Above Confetti rains down as Aaron and I are announced as the winners of *Dancing with the Stars*.

yelling wouldn't work; it would just make me worse. Instead, when I struggled to put everything together, we'd take a short break and then get back to it.

We became very close while working on *Dancing with the Stars*, and we definitely had chemistry on the dance floor. I can see how couples dancing together can end up romantically involved—you spend a lot of time with one another and get very close physically. If you are in a relationship with someone else that has any weaknesses, then the closeness you develop with your dance partner could put that at risk.

However, Aaron and I were both very happy in our relationships with our partners. Marty would fly down from Auckland at the weekend and help out with the kids if needed, then watch the live show from the bleachers. Aaron's wife Jaimee came down for several episodes as well.

So while Aaron and I were close, there was nothing romantic—he was the brother I never had. He had my back, and I trusted him without question. He created an environment in which I felt safe to explore what I could do with my dancing and performing. He would always say, 'Bigger, bigger, BIGGER!' when it came to my movements. Those actions would feel very unnatural to start with, but I did what he asked—it was his job to help me improve each week and he knew what he was doing. Yes, there were tears, but there was never an angry word between us.

It was hard for Aaron because we were rehearsing for up to thirty hours a week, and he hardly saw his family. He would fly home to Auckland on the Monday after the show, spend the day with them and then fly back to Wellington on Tuesday to start rehearsals. For the final two weeks he remained in Wellington the whole time as we needed the Mondays to rehearse. It must have been very lonely for him, staying in a motel and missing his wife and children. But he really was completely dedicated, and I can't thank him enough for everything he did.

A proud moment for the two of us as we pose with the mirror ball trophy.

At the outset, I just wanted to dance well and avoid falling flat on my face on live TV. But as *Dancing with the Stars* progressed, I grew keen to stay as long as I could and raise as much money as possible for the Child Cancer Foundation. In the end, a total of $333,655 was collected for all the charities involved in the second season, and $112,000 of that went to CCF. It felt wonderful to have achieved that.

It wasn't just my charity that did well out of the programme. At the start of the show, the TAB took bets on who was likely to win. My odds were 26–1. Marty made a lot of money!

Chapter Eleven

Dancing with the Stars had consumed such a chunk of my time that, when it finished, I felt a little lost. There were no rehearsals, no costume fittings, no Aaron. I went through a period of readjustment, but one upside was having more time for my children, and for my beautiful man, Marty.

Being able to help the Child Cancer Foundation had been such a positive experience that I offered my services as an ambassador. An ambassador's job is to create awareness of what the organisation does, and with so much competition among charities to raise funds, and only so much money people can give, you need to be able to capture the public's attention.

My role was to work with the media in the lead-up to fundraising efforts, and even though I've never felt comfortable about being a 'celebrity' of sorts, I was glad in this instance that I had a public profile I could use to support such a good cause.

The Child Cancer Foundation Appeal Day was the big fundraiser of the year, and I loved being involved in that. One year we did a trip from Auckland to Tauranga and back again, stopping at each town along the way to collect for the appeal. I was in the same car as food writer and cook Allyson Gofton, whom I had never met before. She was a bundle of energy and extremely entertaining: regaling us with her food stories but also going off on tangents about all sorts of things. I learned a lot!

We'd arrive in places such as Ngatea and Katikati, jump out of our vehicle in the main street and jingle our collection buckets, encouraging the public to contribute. We also got to meet some very brave local children with cancer. Then off we'd go to the next place. The time in the car just flew by because Allyson kept us so enthralled. I have great memories of all the fundraising I was involved in, but that trip was particularly memorable!

In June 2009, my sister Carolyn's daughter Claudia, who was then four, started complaining of a sore stomach. Oddly, she couldn't walk properly on her feet, only on her tippy toes. Claudia was admitted to Starship Children's Hospital with suspected appendicitis, and during the operation the surgeon discovered that her stomach was full of blood. A scan showed that she had a huge haematoma (bruise) on her kidney.

Afterwards the medical staff drew Carolyn and her husband Mark aside and asked who had hit Claudia. It was a shocking question to be asked but, to be fair, the staff were just doing their job. Of course, nobody had hit Claudia; Carolyn and Mark thought the bruise might be something to do with a fall she had had on the jungle gym at kindy that day.

Claudia then had a week of bed rest to allow the haematoma to go away, and once it had healed, a CT scan revealed a 7-cm tumour on the kidney. It appeared that the tumour had ruptured in the fall, leading to the bleeding that the surgeon had found.

The doctors diagnosed a stage III Wilms' tumour, which is a type of kidney cancer. It affects one in every 250,000 children, and we were all shocked to learn that my beautiful niece had it. Carolyn and Mark were devastated as they faced the reality that they could lose their precious daughter. Living with that knowledge was the hardest part of the whole ordeal for them.

But they swiftly went into action mode, drawing strength from one another to be strong for Claudia. As a family, we circled around them to offer our support in any way we could.

I couldn't believe this latest twist of fate: the charity I had chosen for *Dancing with the Stars* three years earlier was now there to help my sister and her family. From my experience with CCF I knew they would be able to offer incredible support, not only to Claudia but also to Carolyn and Mark and their other daughter, Charlotte. CCF is there for the whole family, not just the sick child.

Claudia had six months of chemotherapy, seven radiation sessions, a biopsy and a nephrectomy, which is surgery to remove her kidney. She also had an operation to insert a portacath into a vein in her chest for administering the chemo, followed by more surgery to remove it. And she had a blood transfusion after her kidney removal. That brave wee soul went through so much.

Technically, there is no remission when you have Wilms'. The doctors can say there is 'no evidence of disease' once the kidney and the cancer are gone. Claudia, now twelve, will be checked every year until she turns eighteen. She's such a vibrant and energetic girl; you would never know she has a history of cancer. Like her cousin Jasmine, she is passionate about dance, and she takes part most weekends in competitions. I am so proud of her, and also of Carolyn, Mark and Charlotte for their strength as individuals and their loving bond as a family.

Children like Claudia who go through cancer are given a Bead of Courage to acknowledge their strength and bravery. Each bead represents a treatment (such as chemotherapy, radiotherapy, scans or blood tests), an experience (hair loss, fever, isolation) or a milestone on the journey. The last bead each child receives is a purple heart to signify the end of their treatment.

Claudia received 411 beads from her treatments and experiences. Some children collect thousands of beads; many feel proud of them, and rightly so. Those beads are symbols of their courage. I have huge respect and admiration for all these young people who are grappling with cancer; often they could teach us adults a thing or two about acceptance and getting on with what needs to be done.

Each year, Camp Quality runs a week-long camp for children who are going through cancer treatment or have recently finished.

It provides them with a fun-filled holiday, and gives parents a much-needed break. Each child has a companion assigned to be with them at all times, and those companions are amazingly kind and caring volunteers who give up a week of their time to help these kids.

Mark and Carolyn noticed that for many families, putting the children on the bus to send them off to camp for a week could be quite stressful for all parties. In 2010, they launched the Purple Heart Foundation, which holds an annual day of fun for the children and their families on the day they're heading off to camp. The focus on activities helps to get the kids ready for the trip, and makes it easier for them to say goodbye to their families.

Throughout the year Mark collects goods generously donated by businesses, so that gift packages can be handed out to three deserving families on the day. These have included everything from bikes, televisions and appliances to toys and games.

I've taken part in Purple Heart days as a volunteer, and it is truly uplifting to witness the pleasure these events bring to so many people. Mark and Carolyn put a huge amount of time and energy into making it all happen, and I know they do it as a way of supporting other families who are going through what they went through. It makes me even more proud of them.

I've always said that when something bad happens, good things can manifest from the bad. What happened to Claudia led to so much goodness in the form of the Purple Heart Foundation.

After *Dancing with the Stars*, Marty and I continued our long-distance relationship. He would come down to Wellington every second weekend and I would fly up to Auckland once a month.

Each time I waited to pick him up at our special meeting place at the airport, there would be huge anticipation fluttering inside me. My heart would swell when he jumped in the car beaming that big, beautiful smile. Saying goodbye at the end of the weekend was so hard, and we'd be counting down the days until the next time we saw one another.

When I visited Auckland, we would often end up going to a property Marty had purchased in the Kaipara District in Northland, in an area called Takahoa. He referred to it as 'the farm' as it was surrounded by rolling hills and paddocks full of cows and sheep.

The house was situated high up on a hill overlooking the harbour, and the view was breathtaking. Some mornings we would open the blinds and the whole house was surrounded by mist—it was as though we were floating in the clouds.

The Kaipara area has a strong spiritual history and you can really sense it. Takahoa became our place of freedom and peace, a haven where we could welcome our friends and family as well as cherish time alone together. It was a beautiful spot in which to get to know one another better.

Every time we saw one another, we fell deeper and deeper in love. Marty shared my need for intimacy in a relationship, and we felt that our bond was a meeting of two souls. We both knew that a love on that level is rare and precious, and we were very grateful for it.

We also knew, intuitively, that we wanted to get married. I didn't know where or when the proposal would happen, I just knew that it would.

On a beautiful January evening in 2007, after a day full of love, laughter and fun at Takahoa, we were sitting on the deck admiring the spectacular sunset the Kaipara is renowned for, when deep in my heart, I felt that this was the moment. Wanting it to be perfect, I asked Marty to put our favourite Michael Bublé song on. He went inside, but next thing, blaring out of the outdoor speakers was U2's 'Beautiful Day'.

I couldn't hide my disappointment. But Marty smiled at me.

'Come on, Raine, I know why you wanted me to put that song on, but I have another idea. How about we write down a proposal to each other, and then we'll get up before sunrise tomorrow, go to Mangawhai beach and share what we have written as the sun comes up.'

That put the smile back on my face; it was a great idea. We went our separate ways to write about why we wanted to marry one another. It turned out to be a very meaningful exercise.

The next morning, we woke just before sunrise to the sound of torrential rain. We looked at one another and burst out laughing. A romantic proposal on the beach wasn't going to happen. So we did it right there, in bed, and it was actually beautiful, even if it wasn't the location we'd planned.

In my proposal, I told Marty that I adored him, and felt that he was always with me, even when we were apart. 'You are a part of my soul, the part that brings such joy to my life. I am forever grateful that you love me the way you do; I believe you are indeed my soulmate.'

I told him that his beautiful spirit shone brightly, and asked if he would join me on an amazing journey, walking alongside me as my husband.

As always, Marty was able to write the most incredibly heartfelt words. He told me that I inspired him, and that he had a wonderful and joyous feeling of being 'in-spirit' with me.

'So I, Marty—a man who adores you, respects you, who connects in every way with you, who loves you and is in love with you—ask you, "Will you accept the invitation to partner me in matrimony?"'

Then he went on to say, 'Before you decide, please consider these words: We will grow old together as two young lovers, as two strong pillars standing equally side by side. With certainty and calm, connectedness and care, we will share a joyous journey with our hearts laid bare. Let's follow our bliss but never forget this—life is about one more kiss. Forever, Marty.'

Wow. My answer of course was yes, and so was his. Marty and I were getting married!

The next step was tackling the subject of where we were going to live. Marty was in Auckland, with his daughter, Emma, living nearby. I was in Wellington with Hilton and Jasmine, and their dad was also living in the capital. Whatever we did was going to cause complications.

After much discussion over the course of that year, we decided our home together would be in Auckland. Jasmine was happy to move north with me but Hilton, who was fifteen, wanted to stay in Wellington and live with Murray. I understood why: he was settled there with his friends, his school and his rugby, and he also wanted to be close to his dad. That last reason was wonderful as far as I was concerned—boys of that age need guidance from their fathers more than ever.

'I took a moment to recover, then got up, grabbed the spanner and went back inside—but the look on Marty's face told me something was very wrong.'

Hilton and Murray developed a really close bond through living together during that time, and that has been fantastic for both of them.

Shortly before Christmas 2007, a removal truck packed full of our belongings set off for Auckland. I was about to spend a few quiet moments saying goodbye to my house in Khandallah, which had given me six wonderful years with my children, when Marty noticed that the dryer attachments were still on the wall in the laundry.

I went to get a spanner out of my car, but as I pulled open the car door I had to bend to dodge the branch of an overhanging tree, and I managed to whack my forehead viciously against the door's edge. The pain was so sharp that I dropped to the ground, clutching my head.

I took a moment to recover, then got up, grabbed the spanner and went back inside—but the look on Marty's face told me something was very wrong. It turned out I had a huge haematoma the size of an egg on my forehead. Pretty soon it began to throb painfully, so we left the house, buying ice and painkillers from a service station on the way.

As we turned the car towards Auckland and the long drive ahead of us, I lay back in my seat, head thumping, and realised I hadn't walked through the house to say my final goodbyes. It was disappointing, but on reflection I decided that it was probably just as well: that experience would have been very emotional, especially as I was leaving Hilton behind.

The next day we collected the key for our new home, and moved ourselves in with the help of family and friends. As well as the huge bump on my forehead, I now had two black eyes, and when Marty's friend Wilkie arrived, I could see him looking at me in shock. Marty later told me that when I left the room, Wilkie had a question for him.

'Has Lorraine had her eyes done?'

Oh dear, I thought. If that's what people were likely to think, I would have to avoid going out in public until the bruising had gone down!

It wasn't exactly the way I had imagined returning to my hometown, but never mind. I was with my beautiful man, and I was starting a whole new phase of my life.

Chapter Twelve

No more long-distance phone calls, no more sad goodbyes at airports. It was bliss living with Marty at last and being able to share everyday couple moments without the niggling knowledge that our time together was limited. We could go for long walks, have friends over to share good food and wine, or just hang out at home listening to music or watching movies.

There was definitely a settling-in period because this was so new for us all. I was a little worried about how Jasmine and Emma would get on, but despite the five-year age gap, they hit it off straight away. That was a relief.

I missed Hilton terribly and knew that it was hard for him not having his mum and sister around, but I was glad he was enjoying being with his dad.

Being hopeless romantics, Marty and I wanted to get married on Valentine's Day. I felt we weren't quite ready in February 2008, so we set the date for the following year.

The best thing about living together was having so much time to just *talk*. We could talk to one another about anything and everything, and our relationship continued to grow on a spiritual level.

It wasn't always smooth sailing, though. Whenever we had a disagreement, Marty had a tendency to shut down and withdraw to his man cave for a few days. His ego was usually responsible, because he felt wounded by whatever I had said or done. I couldn't bear it, as silence makes me crazy.

At the time Marty was having sessions with acupuncturist Peter Caughey, who was also a good friend. Marty confided in Peter about this problem, and Peter didn't mince words.

'Marty, you have to stop being a pussy boy,' he advised.

Peter explained to Marty that he wasn't being judged by me when we had these disagreements, and that he shouldn't withdraw. What I needed, Peter said, was for Marty to hold me and say 'I love you' rather than shutting me out.

Marty told me about their discussion, and promised, 'No more pussy boy for me.' After that he worked hard at not taking things to heart and at staying present when issues came up. It really changed our relationship in a positive way.

We also developed a strategy to use when we thought the other might be upset for some reason. We'd say, 'Have you got something in your sack?', meaning 'Is there something you need to talk about?' It was a gentle way of starting a conversation, knowing that you were going to be listened to respectfully. It stopped us from carrying problems around that could have grown worse if we didn't discuss them.

The other phrase important to us was 'in-spirit'. This meant that we were connected by love to one another, and to God, on a spiritual level. It meant no ego, no negativity and no judgement—just pure love and acceptance. These two phrases were tools we found immensely helpful at times when we needed to reconnect.

Those moments of feeling disconnected didn't happen very often. Most of the time we felt blessed because we had found one another. I knew I had been brought back into Marty's life to help him with his spiritual learning, and he was brought to me to show me what it felt like to be loved with an open heart and pure honesty. Marty adored and cherished me, and treated me like his goddess. If I had to pick a song to sum up how he made me feel, it would be Aretha Franklin's '(You Make Me Feel Like) A Natural Woman'.

Marty and I were so close that we were convinced we had shared previous lives, and we were constantly seeing signs of a history together. Interestingly, on the day I won Miss Universe—11 July 1983—Marty was experiencing a huge personal achievement: scoring his maiden first-class century for New Zealand against a county side at Lord's in England.

Our paths were meant to cross, and I couldn't wait until we officially became husband and wife.

On the morning of 14 February 2009, I was woken at around 4 a.m. by an unmistakable noise. I jolted upright in bed as if possessed, and woke up Marty.

'Please tell me that's not rain!' I implored.

'I'm sorry, it is,' said Marty.

I had a wee tantrum. It was not meant to rain on our wedding day! The ceremony was being held on a private pink-sand beach alongside the beautiful house in Omaha where we had spent our first weekend together, and the reception was supposed to be beside the pool. If the torrential rain didn't stop we were going to get drenched.

After a while I calmed down and reminded myself of the most important thing: we were sharing our commitment to one another with our family and friends. The weather didn't matter.

'Okay, time for plan B,' I said to Marty.

Wise words, but unfortunately, there was no plan B ready and waiting. The weather had been hot and sunny all week, so we'd expected it to be the same for our wedding.

When it became clear that the downpour wasn't going to relent, our families helped us move everything inside. Marty's sister Deb, who is a very talented interior designer, did an amazing job of setting the scene, arranging Singapore orchids and frangipani around the house so that it looked absolutely beautiful.

We had seventy guests for the wedding, most of whom were bused up from Auckland, and when they arrived I could tell they felt sorry for us because the weather was so bad. But their energy was loving and heartfelt, and it was almost as if they were saying, 'We don't care, we are just so happy to see you two get married.'

We turned tradition on its head when it came to our outfits.

Top Wedding-day cuddles with Mum and Noel (left) and my beautiful daughter Jasmine. All wedding photos by Todd Eyre and Ross Coffey for *The Australian Women's Weekly*.

Above The two gorgeous men in my life: Hilton and Marty.

Top My Wellington girlfriends were so happy for me.

Above Dave Morris sings 'You're Beautiful' (left) and Frances touches our hearts with her reading.

Marty, Hilton, Jasmine and Emma all wore white, while my dress was aquamarine. At my age (I was forty-four) I didn't want to wear white or cream, and instead chose a colour that would reflect the sea. The dress, designed by Jane Yeh, was made of silk chiffon and organza, and sprinkled with tiny Swarovski crystals. I felt wonderful in it. Of course, I knew that it didn't really matter what I wore; what mattered was that I was marrying my soulmate.

We wrote our own vows, and spoke from the heart about the depth of our love. We promised to love one another well; I told Marty that my love for him and our children would always be the most important thing in my life, while he vowed to be my husband for life.

Marty made a lovely toast to my dad, Lloyd, and to his own dad, Dave, who had died of cancer in 2000. In his speech, Marty talked about that night at the Clearwater Resort when he'd played James Blunt's 'You're Beautiful' through the wall in a bid to woo me—and scare off my blind date.

'He had no chance with my Romeo act,' Marty told everyone.

Marty's old school friend from his Auckland Grammar days, Dave Morris, sang 'You're Beautiful' to us, sealing a truly special moment. And my dear friend, Frances Jones, delivered an emotional reading.

Our wedding could not have been more wonderful. Our cherished friends and family were all there, including Marty's brother Jeff, who flew over from his home in Florida, as well as Jean, China and lots of my close girlfriends from Wellington. Aaron Gilmore and his wife Jaimee were among the guests, along with Marty's sporting mates Grant Fox, Ian Smith and Mark Greatbatch.

There was just so much love, and I felt truly blessed.

And, wouldn't you know it, by the late afternoon, once the service was over, the sun came out! Never mind. At least it meant we could dance out by the pool—a perfect end to a perfect day.

It always warmed my heart
to see the bond between
Marty and Emma.

I knew for sure that I had fallen truly, deeply and head over heels in love with Marty when I first saw him with his daughter, Emma. He was a natural father; gentle, funny and patient. He adored her and, whenever she was with him, he gave her his whole attention.

Watching Marty with Emma made me want to have a child with him, and fortunately he felt the same way. Just as being a mother meant everything to me, being a father was the best thing he had ever done. It seemed so right to bring a child into this world from a place of pure, 'grown-up' love. The problem was that we were well and truly grown-ups: I was forty-four and Marty was forty-six, and we knew that conception and pregnancy might be difficult.

We had first started trying in 2008. Not long afterwards, Marty was asked to be a part of the first IPL cricket series in India as a chief cricket officer. He was going to be away for six weeks, and I was planning on visiting him twice during his time there. Just days before I was meant to fly over for my first visit, I realised that my period was late, so I took a pregnancy test. To my absolute delight, it was positive.

I called Marty, but before I even had the chance to say anything he spoke up.

'You're pregnant, aren't you?'

That's how close we were; he just knew.

Marty was thrilled, and agreed with my doctor that I should cancel my trip to India because it was too risky to travel at this very early stage. So I stayed home, and over the next couple of weeks I had blood tests to check how the pregnancy was going.

My heart plummeted when I was given the early results. The levels of pregnancy hormones in my blood were not very high, which meant the pregnancy might not be viable and was unlikely to advance. In other words, there was a good chance this baby wasn't going to make it.

A little later, another blood test showed that there was no longer a pregnancy. I called Marty in tears to tell him the news.

'Get on the next plane and come to India,' he told me. He was as upset as I was, and we grieved together.

We kept trying for a baby, and after our wedding we decided to see a fertility specialist. He told us that I could give fertility treatment a go, but the chances of it working were slim because of my age.

Despite the specialist's gloomy prognosis, I was still hopeful. My grandmother had given birth to my mother, the last of her thirteen children, when she was forty-seven. If she could have a baby in her forties, why couldn't I?

Marty had a test and it showed no problems in his department. Being an eternal optimist, I started the treatment, which involved taking drugs to boost ovulation.

Unfortunately, the pills turned me into a crazy lady. They wreaked havoc on my hormones and made my abdomen feel like it was going to explode. I just had to grit my teeth and remind myself that hopefully it would be worth it.

On a certain day of my cycle each month, I would go to the clinic to have a vaginal scan, which showed how many eggs my ovaries had released. In spite of his earlier negativity, the specialist actually got excited when he looked at the ultrasound images.

'Your body has taken to the medication very well,' he told me. 'You've released a lot of eggs. I have to tell you, with what I'm seeing, there's a possibility you could have twins or triplets.'

Oh my goodness, I thought. I was thrilled that the pills were working, but two or three babies? We only wanted one! Still, we would be happy with whatever we were given.

So, every month I would go for my scan and I'd be told there were eggs that could potentially become embryos. *This is it, I'm going to get pregnant*, I would think. And then every month I would get my period. The disappointment caused real pain—I felt like I'd lost a baby, even though there was nothing there to lose. I wanted a child so much, and every month I'd end up grieving.

Eventually we had to accept that we were not going to have a baby. I could not keep taking the medication; it affected me badly and made me moody and emotional. We saw this as a sign that a baby just wasn't meant to be, but it took me a long time to come to terms with it. Right up until I was about forty-seven, part of me was still hopeful that by some fluke I would follow in my grandmother's footsteps and get pregnant at that late stage.

But it didn't happen, and I had to let go of that dream.

A few months after I lost the baby, my ex-husband Murray came to visit me in Auckland, which I thought was a little strange as it wasn't something he usually did.

'Lorraine, I have some news, and I want to share it with you personally before you hear it from anyone else,' Murray said.

He told me that his partner, Mariska (now his wife), was three months pregnant. I realised that if things had been different, we would have been pregnant at the same time.

The loss of my own baby didn't stop me feeling happy for Murray and Mariska. Their daughter, Hanalei, named after their favourite place in Hawaii, is a sweet girl, and Hilton and Jasmine love her to bits. I feel a real connection with her, too, as though she's one of mine.

About a year after my miscarriage, I saw a clairvoyant who confirmed what I was trying to come to terms with—that I wasn't going to have a baby with Marty.

'I can't tell you why you haven't been given a baby, but I'm being told that there is a good reason why, and you will understand one day,' she said.

Now I do know why. Marty and I wanted a baby so much, not only because we hoped to create a new life out of our deep love, but also because we wanted to share the parenting experience together. But, if I'd had the baby I lost, today I would be raising a nine-year-old child on my own.

I think that is why a baby never manifested for us: because of what was to come for Marty.

Chapter Thirteen

Other than our sadness over not being able to have a baby, married life with Marty was heavenly. We had a beautiful home, across the road from a park and just a short walk to a beach, and we were happy there together. Jasmine lived with us full-time and Emma came to stay often, while Hilton visited from Wellington whenever he could.

My career was suffering, though, because the move from Wellington to Auckland had meant leaving behind a successful image consulting business, which I had built up purely on word of mouth. In Auckland, there were so many more people working in my field. The city had changed dramatically since I last lived and worked there twenty-two years earlier, and the fashion industry had a very 'cool' feeling to it, which I wasn't used to. It all felt very new and foreign to me, unlike relaxed and safe Wellington.

I knew I would have to start again from scratch, which is not easy when your self-assurance has taken a hit. But I persevered, because I love what I do. Being an image consultant does include advising women on the colours and styles that suit them, but there is a lot more to it than that. My work goes to a much deeper level.

Women sometimes lose their way when it comes to knowing who they are and how they should be dressing, and that can lead to a loss of confidence. I believe that it's important to connect to your inner self, so you understand who you are and what makes you special. If you don't do that, you'll never feel confident, no matter how fabulous your outfit is.

My work has evolved to help women find their essence, and to be happy and comfortable with who they are. I've had really lovely feedback from my clients, and I find it so rewarding to be part of a process that leads to these ladies blossoming and discovering their true selves.

I had also been acting as a spokesperson for various products, but that work had just about completely dried up.

After I won *Dancing with the Stars*, an advertising agency had arranged for me to be the spokesperson for an exercise machine called Power Plate. The account manager who suggested me for the one-year role was Lou Henderson, a friend I'd got to know through my first husband. Lou's husband at the time was a close friend of Murray's, and we girls had had our first babies together.

Lou was now working in advertising in Auckland. Feeling that I could use some help in lining up jobs, I called her and arranged to have lunch.

'So, how's work going?' she asked me.

'Actually, it's not,' I told her.

Lou was shocked, and within seconds she'd come up with a host of ideas for companies and products she thought would be a good fit. She understood something that was very important to me—that the fit had to be right. I knew I could never associate myself with anything I didn't trust or totally believe in; having integrity is vital to me.

As she reeled off a list of possibilities, I felt a burst of excitement. This was just what I needed.

'Lou, would you like to become my manager?' I asked.

'Really?' She had never managed anyone before.

'What you just shared with me is perfect; you'd be a fantastic manager.'

She thought about it and decided that she'd love to take on the role.

Getting Lou on board was one of the best things I ever did. At that stage she'd had twenty-five years' experience in advertising, and she was well respected and trusted in the industry. She

A recent snap of me with my talented friend and manager Louise Henderson.

understood how it all worked, and I knew I would be in very capable and efficient hands.

It was the beginning of a wonderful partnership—not to mention friendship—that continues to this day. Lou also became Marty's manager. He affectionately named her S.A.H., for Super Agent Henderson.

Thanks to Lou, I ended up working with Living Nature, a 100-percent-natural skincare company based in Kerikeri in Northland. They'd never had a 'face' to promote their products before, and my job was to encourage women to take their first step towards using natural skincare. It was definitely the perfect fit for me, and the timing couldn't have been better: at forty-five I was starting to do some soul-searching about the ageing process.

Botox was the buzzword at the time, and some of my friends were using it. I wondered if this was a path I should be going down. Around the same time, I was approached about being involved with an appearance medicine company, and I attended a demonstration of the various products and procedures used. I felt a bit queasy watching the video clips and seeing the before and after photos, and decided then and there that I wanted to age naturally. I wasn't the right person to be promoting that company.

I have come to understand that ageing is something you can either fear and fight, or you can accept and go with. I have chosen the latter path. I don't want to be chained to a mirror and fretting about my wrinkles for the rest of my life. Actually, I think lines around the eyes are beautiful—they are a legacy of all the times we've laughed during our precious life journey.

It doesn't matter how many wrinkles I have; they are just a part of me and my history. I think the inner spiritual connection I have developed over the years has helped me to realise that. What really matters is how much love I have in my heart for myself and others.

For me, good health and vitality is the most important aspect of appearance. I started making conscious decisions about the food I was eating and the products I was putting on my skin, and I couldn't believe it when I read that a woman can apply around 168 chemicals to her skin in an average day. I decided not to do that.

So working with Living Nature appealed to me instantly, but before I signed up for a three-year partnership, I went to their premises in Kerikeri and saw for myself how their products were made. It was fascinating to witness their exceptionally high factory standards, and to learn about the amazing properties of New Zealand plants—eighty percent of which cannot be found anywhere else in the world—and how they benefit the skin. I bet you never knew that harakeke flax is up to three times more hydrating than aloe vera!

I fell in love with the whole concept of natural skincare, and working for such an authentic New Zealand company was a dream come true.

We kicked off my involvement with Living Nature by shooting an advertising campaign in a series of stunning locations in the far north, including Hokianga, Matauri Bay and Te Ngaere Bay. I was able to choose the team for the shoot, which I appreciated. It's so important that there is good energy when you're doing something like a photo shoot, and that comes down to the people involved.

The team I brought together included photographer Monty Adams, make-up artist Aimie Fiebig and fashion stylist Sonia Greenslade. I've said before that Monty is my favourite photographer: he has a remarkable ability to make women look beautiful in his shots, and he's always fun to work with. Aimie weaves magic with make-up and hair, and has a real understanding of working with more mature skin. And Sonia instinctively knows which clothes will suit me. Besides being cool and talented, she loves to have a good laugh, too.

The shoot with those three pros and the team from Living Nature was one of the best work experiences I've ever had. We shot the images over several days in gorgeous natural locations, including secluded beaches and an ancient forest.

One of the best shots we got had me posing on the beach

with the Living Nature logo drawn into the sand (I'd love to say it was my creative effort, but in fact the logo was drawn by Brett Alexander from Living Nature). It was the very end of the day and we were about to lose the sun. Monty was yelling, 'Quick, we've only got a few minutes!' as we sprinted down the beach to the designated spot. He threw me a piece of driftwood and said, 'Do your thing, Lorraine!'

Afterwards we all collapsed laughing, but we got the shot! I love it because it looks so natural, perfectly representing Living Nature's products and philosophy.

Among the things I did for Living Nature was a tour at the end of 2010, which involved travelling to Christchurch, Wellington, Hamilton and Auckland and speaking to a room full of people about what authentic beauty meant to me. A panel of experts then answered questions, and after the presentation I would talk to the guests, which was often a highlight. I met some lovely people.

Out of all the presentations I did on that tour, the one in Auckland was the most challenging for me. The energy in the room was really low and I couldn't sense the same buzzy excitement that had been present in the other cities. I wondered why it was so different to the rest of the country. Did women in Auckland not really want to hear a message about natural, authentic beauty? Were they more interested in appearance medicine? I don't know what the reason was, but the evening definitely didn't flow as well as the others and it was a disappointment.

By contrast, our presentation in Christchurch had been particularly successful, and a joy to be involved in. While I was there I was interviewed by a local TV channel, CTV, on their morning show. It went well, and the producer Donna Manning was super positive, asking me if I would come back in the New Year to be on the show again. I was only too happy to do it, and we organised a return trip for 23 February 2011. But I never made it. On 22 February a devastating earthquake struck Christchurch, killing 185 people. Sadly, the lovely Donna was one of them.

Striking the perfect shot
for Living Nature. Photo
by Monty Adams.

I had a wonderful time working for Living Nature, and I was very sad when it ended after three years. New management had a different vision about what they wanted when it came to promoting their products, and my contract wasn't renewed.

I still use natural products and I know my skin reaps the benefits. The way you live your life also shows in your skin—when I have one too many wines, my skin is puffy the morning after and takes a few days to look hydrated again. I also believe your skin reflects what is going on in your heart. A happy heart equates to a radiant face, and that's something appearance medicine can't do.

Being 'famous' is a double-edged sword. It has given me many amazing experiences, introduced me to some wonderful people, and helped me win earning opportunities such as my contract with Living Nature. But being recognised is still something I struggle with, even all these years after winning Miss Universe.

I was in Melbourne a few months back, walking along a city street, when I heard a woman I'd just passed say, 'That was Lorraine Downes.' It gave me a shock, partly because I was overseas, but also because my public profile isn't particularly high at the moment. The reality is that once you have been in the public eye, some people won't forget.

When I came back to New Zealand after my year as Miss Universe, I naïvely thought my life would return to the way it was before I won. It took time to dawn on me that losing my anonymity was part of the package.

The thing I find awkward is being acknowledged when I'm doing something very ordinary like going to the supermarket or the movies. I get it on the phone, too: when I give my name I'll hear, 'Oh, are you *the* Lorraine Downes, the beauty queen?'

Then there are those truly awful times when I've just wanted to dig a hole and bury myself. Like the time on a plane when my baby was having a screaming meltdown, or when my toddler announced in a very loud voice, 'Mummy, I've done poos!' Those situations are embarrassing enough; imagine what it is like when everyone knows who you are. There are just some things that you want to remain private, but if you have a public profile, it seems nothing is off limits as far as the media is concerned. I do understand the human interest in well-known people's lives, but that doesn't make it any easier to handle.

When Murray and I were separating, a journalist turned up at our home to try to get a response from us. And when Marty was ill, I had media calling to get an update on his condition. Sometimes it seems the best way to handle it is to put out a press release, so the correct information can be given and we can be left alone to deal with the situation.

If there's one thing I've learned over the years from having a public profile, it's that what gets printed about famous people is not necessarily true. Idle gossip can be toxic and lead to ideas of the 'truth' that are very far removed from what has really happened. As a result, if I haven't seen something with my own eyes, or been told about it directly by the person involved, I reserve the right not to believe it.

So, if I'm not a fan of the public attention I get, why have I appeared on magazine covers and shared stories about myself at various stages of my life?

That's a good question.

There are a couple of reasons why I've done this. One is that doing publicity is often part of my contract with the company I'm representing or the project I'm working on, such as Living Nature or *Dancing with the Stars*.

Another is that it gives me the chance to talk about charities I am involved with, and create awareness of the work they do.

And then there have been times when I've felt that sharing some aspect of my life may be useful for readers who are going through the same thing. For example, when I turned fifty I did a magazine story about how I was coping with reaching this milestone; my hope was that the mindset I had developed (embracing ageing, rather than dreading it) might get other women thinking.

I've never done any media purely for the sake of my ego—that is just not me. According to the feedback I've had from readers, the things I've shared in magazine articles have been received positively, and occasionally I have been told that my story has helped or inspired someone on their personal life journey.

It is always nice to hear this, but to be honest, if I had the choice I would rather not have a public profile. I look at really famous people like Victoria Beckham and Nicole Kidman, and I don't know how they do it. They can't step out of their front door without their every move being followed. Everything they do is analysed; judgements are passed all the time on how they look. I don't envy them one bit.

One of the most difficult things for me to live with is the 'beauty queen' tag. That pageant was in 1983, more than thirty years ago, and yet I'm still often introduced as 'Lorraine Downes, who won Miss Universe'. With that tends to come a deep scrutiny. Recently, a woman introduced me to her children as a former Miss Universe, and I could tell by the looks on their faces they were thinking, *Really? Her?* I don't blame them, I'd have been disbelieving too—I certainly didn't look like a Miss Universe that day.

But the main reason I am sensitive about this label is that I have gone on to achieve a lot more since that long-ago win. I have never wanted Miss Universe to define me. For me, my greatest achievement has been raising my two wonderful children.

While I don't want to be known only as a former Miss Universe, I do appreciate that winning changed my life, and that it made New Zealanders feel proud that one of their own had been successful.

In 2013, Lou Henderson reminded me that it was the thirtieth anniversary of me being crowned Miss Universe.

'What's happened to your crown and your sash?' she asked. 'Where's the trophy and the gown you wore?'

'The crown and the sash are in the garage somewhere,' I said. 'And as for the trophy and the gown . . . I thought I'd lost those years ago, but they've just turned up again.'

I was very moved by the exhibition that Te Papa put together to mark the thirtieth anniversary of my Miss Universe win. Photo by the Museum of New Zealand Te Papa Tongarewa.

op My typical Saturday
ıorning for many years:
ccompanying Hilton to
ugby games.

elow Me and my darling
asmine on a holiday in Fiji.
Ve both love the water.

Left My first live performance on *Dancing with the Stars* with professional dance partner Aaron Gilmore. He warned me that my costumes would get even shorter as the series progressed! All *DWTS* photos by Neil Mackenzie.

Below In show five all the remaining couples performed a group dance, the Viennese waltz. By this stage I was finally starting to get the better of my nerves.

Aaron and I scored a 10
for our rumba in show six.
This was the red dress that
Marty took a shine to!

Top Chatting with the show's host Jason Gunn after performing our first round of dances in the final.

Above Our final dance (left) was a freestyle number. We were both beaming as we posed afterwards with the trophy.

Opposite Marty and I married on Valentine's Day, 14 February 2009. All wedding photos by Todd Eyre and Ross Coffey for *The Australian Women's Weekly*.

Top Posing with Marty's family on our wedding day: his mum Audrey, brother Jeff and sister Deb.

Right My close friend Louise Calabro came over from Los Angeles to share in the big day.

Opposite I was honoured when the *Weekly* asked me to appear on the cover of this special issue in 2012. The photographer and I spent hours seeking the perfect shot. Photo by Monty Adams for the *New Zealand Woman's Weekly*.

NEW ZEALAND
Woman's Weekly
June 25, 2012
$4.10 (incl GST)
COLLECTOR'S EDITION
80th
BIRTHDAY
ISSUE
Our most inspiring women

Top Emma's eleventh birthday in 2014 was a stunning day, and Marty managed a walk to the top of Mount Maunganui with us. Of course he's wearing his favourite colour, orange.

Left Me and my beautiful man during our happy holiday in Bali.

Murray had been clearing out his storage cupboard and had found both items in a box. I was chuffed, as I had thought they'd been lost forever in one of our house moves.

Lou wasn't impressed by the fact that I kept such special items of memorabilia packed away in the garage.

'It's not just a part of your history; it's part of New Zealand's history,' she said. 'You should do something with them.'

With that in mind, she approached the Museum of New Zealand Te Papa Tongarewa, and asked if they would be interested in exhibiting my Miss Universe items, or at least storing them properly for me.

Te Papa's response was extremely positive—in fact they suggested holding an exhibition to mark the thirtieth anniversary of my win.

I packaged up the dress, crown, sash and trophy and sent them down to museum staff in Wellington. I also filmed a video clip for the exhibition, in which I reflected on my experience. It was surprisingly emotional for me, remembering everything I had been through and how it had changed my life.

Lou and I flew down to Wellington for the opening of the exhibition, which featured a moving Maori blessing. I was totally overwhelmed when I saw what the museum had done with my items. All the pieces were beautifully arranged, and the display included video footage from the competition as well as the clip I had made. It was much more than I had expected and I was very grateful to Te Papa, and to Lou for coming up with the idea.

The exhibition was meant to run for six months, but that period was extended due to public interest. It still seems strange to me that I'm considered a cultural icon of sorts!

Thanks to being seen as a part of New Zealand's history, I was asked to be on the cover of a special issue of the *New Zealand Woman's Weekly*, marking the magazine's eightieth anniversary. I'd appeared in the magazine many times since my very first cover back in 1983. As well as celebrating eighty years of publication, they told me that they wanted to pay tribute to inspirational New Zealand women. It was a huge honour to be asked to be on the cover.

For the photo shoot I wore a stunning jade-green dress designed by the very talented Tanya Carlson. While I may look very relaxed in the photos—in which the dress is flowing around me and my arms are draped over a giant gold number 80—in fact I was in agony. I had to stand in very high heels, holding the pose for hours so that Monty Adams could get the perfect shot. There were so many components that had to be exactly right: the dress had to flow in a certain way, my arms and legs had to be positioned just so, my hair had to look perfect, the lighting had to be spot on and the props had to stay upright—in spite of the wind machine set up to blow my dress out.

'They say the camera doesn't lie, but it did in this case. I'm smiling in the pictures but my body was screaming in pain.'

They say the camera doesn't lie, but it did in this case. I'm smiling in the pictures but my body was screaming in pain. When I woke up the next day, my back was shot.

The *Woman's Weekly* held a party to celebrate the eightieth anniversary and launch the special issue. I was asked to speak at the event, and to wear the dress from the cover shoot. While it looked gorgeous in the photos, it wasn't really the best thing for me to wear out in public: I don't have the bust to hold up a dress with those kind of straps. The top kept sliding down, exposing my padded strapless bra, and Lou, who'd accompanied me to the party, was constantly throwing me looks to say, 'Hitch the dress up, Lorraine, your bra's showing.'

I wasn't the only one having underwear issues. My good friend, broadcaster Kerre McIvor (then Woodham), who was wearing a dress the same colour as mine, confided how uncomfortable she was in her Nancy Ganz shapewear.

'Take them off,' I counselled her. 'You need to be comfortable.'

She followed my advice, and thanked me later that evening. I'm a big believer in the importance of being comfortable in what you're wearing; it was just a shame that I couldn't relax in the dress I had on.

I also couldn't help wishing that they'd asked Kerre, who is a brilliant speaker and very, very funny, to give the speech. I hadn't done any public speaking for ages, and as the time approached for me to stand up in front of the crowd of hundreds, I was feeling really scared. The place was packed with people whom I respected and admired. It seemed that every New Zealand media person I had ever seen on TV was there, along with familiar faces from our fashion, politics, publishing, acting and music industries. I started panicking about my speech, worrying that it was going to fall flat.

I took myself off to the bathroom and read through my notes, and all I could think was, *This isn't funny enough; it isn't clever enough*. All these negative thoughts were rushing through my head, and I was really fearful. So I did the only thing I could: I took a deep breath and prayed to God to help me relax and speak from my heart.

As always, God came through for me. I was able to get through my speech, talking fondly about how I loved to read copies of the magazine in the sun porch of my nana's house when I was a little girl. I think I did okay. But I'm not planning on giving up image consulting to be an MC or a public speaker, that's for sure.

Chapter Fourteen

I shouldn't have worried about my image consultancy business: by 2011 it was thriving, and I was about to launch a new project called The Gift. This was a section on my website that would cover subjects I was interested in such as health, family, beauty, fashion and spiritual enlightenment. I saw it as a way of inspiring women and helping them to find their true essence. I believe that everyone has a gift to share with the world, and encouraging others to find theirs is a gift I can offer.

I'd had a logo designed and started posting motivational quotes on The Gift page of my website. I had plans for a possible TV series further down the track in which I would interview inspirational people, including those who had helped me along my own path. I was very excited about it, but unfortunately it never really got off the ground. I couldn't give it the time and effort it required, because two of the most precious people in my life needed my energy instead.

Shortly before Christmas 2011 my mum, Glad, read an article in a magazine about journalist Helena McAlpine, who had breast cancer, and it prompted her to check her own breasts. Mum was seventy-six at the time, and she had previously had regular mammograms as part of the government's BreastScreen Aotearoa programme, which funds mammograms for women aged forty-five to sixty-nine. Mum had assumed that because the free screening finished at sixty-nine, women over that age had little risk of getting breast cancer and it was not necessary to continue checking her breasts.

But she did a thorough self-examination anyway, and found a lump the size of a golf ball that had been pretty well hidden.

A biopsy was carried out on the lump, and she received the result a few days before Christmas. It was negative, which was a huge relief for Mum as well as my sisters and me. Christmas that year was celebrated with a tremendous sense of gratitude.

However, in the New Year Mum had a follow-up appointment with the specialist, who didn't like the feel of the lump and wanted it tested again. This time the results were different: it turned out the lump was cancerous. Mum was told she needed a mastectomy followed by chemotherapy and radiation. The treatment had to be aggressive because of the size of the lump and the fact that it had been there for some time.

The diagnosis was devastating. Mum is the last of a family of thirteen children, many of whom had passed away from different forms of cancer. We had thought she was doing so well to have reached seventy-six and bypassed this hideous disease. And now, it seemed so wrong that at her age she was facing some very invasive medical procedures. My sisters and I vowed that we would be there with her through every stage, so she never had to take a single step on this terrifying journey without at least one of us beside her. Sue, Jenny, Carolyn and I had always been close, but supporting our adored mum brought us even closer.

Mum opted for a double mastectomy because she was worried about the cancer showing up in the other breast, and because she didn't want to be lopsided. The day before the surgery she asked me if I would take a photo of her that showed her breasts, so I did. She is such a strong and brave woman, my mum.

Throughout the eight months of chemotherapy and radiation that followed, one of us girls was always sitting with Mum during her treatment. It was so hard seeing our mother, who had always been our nurturer and protector, that ill and weak. She lost her hair,

Gettin a hug from my
darling mum Glad.

and when I took her to get a wig I could see her vulnerability as she tried them on. She chose one she was happy with, but hardly wore it in the end; she preferred the lovely fabric turbans I got her from Kaus. The turbans looked great and felt so soft on her head.

As the treatment wore on, we never once heard Mum complain or say 'Why me?' She never felt sorry for herself. When she was feeling awful, she would think of her granddaughter Claudia, who had battled cancer three years earlier.

'Claudia was so brave—if she can get through this, so can I,' she'd say.

The most heartbreaking moment for me came a few days after one of Mum's chemo treatments. She was lying on her bed, her head hairless and her body weak and frail.

'Lorraine, I can't talk, so it's best that you go so I can rest,' she said to me.

I felt so helpless. I wanted to wrap her in my arms and perform some kind of loving magic that would make everything all right.

She gave us a terrible fright on one occasion when her temperature soared to over 40°C. When you're having chemo your immune system is weakened, so her body was struggling to combat the high fever. She was admitted to hospital and had to fight for her life, but she survived.

Taking one day at a time, Mum came through all of her treatment. And after that, she had to go back to hospital for another (non-cancer-related) surgery that had been put on hold. Watching the way she handled herself through these frightening times filled me with enormous respect for my mother.

Today Mum is fit and well, and cancer-free. She had knee surgery in 2015, and recuperating from that was tough—but she's glad she did it because it means she can still get out and about. She recently turned eighty-one, and continues to inspire us all with her bravery, wisdom and love for her family.

As a result of what Mum went through, I decided to switch from being an ambassador for the Child Cancer Foundation to being one for the Breast Cancer Foundation New

Zealand. One of my main motivations was to get the message out there about the importance of checking for cancer once you're over the free-screening cut-off age of sixty-nine. Research shows that women are actually more at risk of getting breast cancer in their seventies than they are in their fifties, and I thought all women needed to be aware of that.

The Breast Cancer Foundation asked if Mum and I would help with an awareness campaign by making a video that could be shown in rest homes and similar venues. In the video, I interviewed Mum, asking her questions about her cancer experience. We also did a photo shoot together and an interview on one of the TV stations.

I had to push Mum into this because she hates having her photo taken—let alone speaking on camera—but even though it was challenging for her, she was a real trouper. She felt strongly about making women aware that you still need to be vigilant about your breast health over the age of seventy.

The foundation also started a petition asking the government to extend the cut-off age for the free breast-screening programme from sixty-nine to seventy-four. In April 2016, I travelled to Wellington to present the petition of 10,000 signatures to Labour MP Jacinda Ardern (then in opposition) so she could table it in Parliament. Jacinda is a big supporter of breast cancer initiatives and we were hopeful that the petition would gain some traction.

When Jacinda became prime minister in October 2017, one of the first things she did was announce that the coalition government would progressively raise the cut-off age for free breast screening to seventy-four. Mum and I were absolutely thrilled to hear the news. The Breast Cancer Foundation released a press statement saying that this move would save many lives.

'This decision is important not just for women, but for all New Zealanders, many of whom will now get to enjoy their mothers, sisters, aunt and grandmothers for longer,' said chief executive Evangelia Henderson.

In their Facebook post announcing the news, the foundation kindly thanked me and Mum for getting the ball rolling on the petition. It was nice to be acknowledged, but I was just happy that I had been able to get something done about a cause I felt

Accepting flowers from the Breast Cancer Foundation's chief executive Evangelia 'Van' Henderson.

strongly about. This was one of those times when I felt there was a good reason why I had a public profile; why I had won Miss Universe all those years ago. It had given me a voice, and that voice had helped to make a change for the better. For that, I am very thankful.

Many years earlier, when Marty and I had met up at the Massey Memorial in Wellington the day before our disastrous date, I had taken another item with me besides that mini bottle of champagne: a book called *The Secret Language of Birthdays*. It describes people and their personalities according to their birthdate, and I have found it uncannily accurate.

My birthdate is the Day of Buoyant Optimism, which is spot on for me. Marty's was the Day of the Restless Soul, and when he read that, he smiled.

'I guess that's true,' he said.

Once I got to know him, I couldn't believe how correct that description of him was. He could be very restless at times, and I'm sure that came from the fact that he had an incredibly active mind. He was a great thinker, and that got him in trouble sometimes because he couldn't turn off his thoughts.

His restlessness was evident in a 2012 photo shoot we did together to build awareness of the Variety Club's Heart to Heart Kids campaign, which aimed to raise funds for kids who were gifted in some way but couldn't pursue their talent for financial reasons. The campaign encouraged people to host a social get-together with friends to raise money. We jumped on board because we had kids with passions for dance and sport, and we knew how costly those endeavours could be.

For the photo shoot, we had to pretend we were barbecuing. After ten shots had been taken Marty called out, 'Great, got it!'

Everyone else knew we hadn't got it at all, but he didn't realise that it can take around fifty photos to get 'the' shot. I guess that's why I was the model and he wasn't. By the end of that shoot, the tongs he was wielding were getting tapped on the barbecue in frustration!

That was the only time we joined forces as a couple for a campaign (unless you count that hilarious in-house video for National Bank back in the early nineties). While we loved doing things together, we kept our professional lives, and some of our personal interests, separate. I had my tango and he had his golf. I did my image consultancy work and he worked at Sky, producing rugby coverage.

'We supported one another in all our ventures, but I had my doubts when Marty raised the subject of returning to cricket in the middle of 2011 . . . He said it was because he wanted a challenge, which was typical of him.'

We supported one another in all our ventures, but I had my doubts when Marty raised the subject of returning to cricket in the middle of 2011. He told me he was considering playing again, firstly at club level and then perhaps for Auckland.

'If you feel this is what you want to do, then go for it,' I told him. But privately I was thinking, *Where is this coming from and why does he feel the need to play cricket again after sixteen years away from the sport?*

He said it was because he wanted a challenge, which was typical of him. He was at a stage in his life where he needed to push himself.

Marty had had to give up international cricket because of a bad knee, but a successful operation had stabilised it. Tests showed his eyesight was stronger, his hand reactions were faster, and his balance and movement were better than they had been when he was tested nineteen years earlier, back in 1992.

I watched as he put this idea into action, setting up media interviews to explain why he was returning to the sport. We had different views on how to deal with the media—he liked to talk to them; I didn't. As expected, there was a lot of interest in his comeback, and the spotlight was really on him to see whether he would achieve his goal of getting back into first-class cricket or whether he would fail.

I wished that Marty could have made his return to cricket without the media—and now the public—watching his every move. But of course it was very naïve of me to think that one of this country's most successful cricketers could walk out onto a cricket pitch one Saturday and go unnoticed.

The move was going to mean a lot of pressure on him once again, and my gut was uneasy. But I didn't say anything as I knew it wouldn't help him with what he was trying to achieve. I just had to let things take their course.

He was clearly enjoying the preparation and getting fit, which was wonderful to see. But something just didn't feel right.

After a couple of games, I got a text from Marty saying 'It's all over'. His thumb had been broken in four places when he was taking a catch. It was a very complex fracture and Marty was devastated, because it had well and truly put an end to him playing cricket.

I was sorry he had to go through that, but I couldn't help thinking there was a reason why he'd broken his thumb. His comeback cricketing career just wasn't meant to be.

Marty also loved being challenged when it came to his work. He'd been at Sky TV for sixteen years—thirteen of them as a full-time employee—and in that time he had introduced some highly successful sporting concepts, including Cricket Max and coverage of First XV rugby. He was intelligent, creative and insightful; always thinking ahead because he didn't want Sky's programmes to become stale.

But in 2012, his department at Sky was undergoing a shake-up as a result of new management. In September of that year, he was told he was one of four executive producers whose jobs were being discontinued due to restructuring. There was another producing job he could apply for, but it would mean half the salary.

He got this news the day before his fiftieth birthday, and it was obviously a very stressful time for him. We'd booked a trip to Bali, leaving a couple of days later, and that timing proved to be perfect: our break away would give him the chance to do some thinking.

I couldn't wait to share Bali with Marty, who had only been once before. I just love the place—the warm weather, the lush vegetation, the delicious food, and especially the kind and gentle people. There is a spiritual element to Bali that ignites all your senses. From the smell of incense burning around the clock and the Balinese music chiming away in the background to the daily offerings to the gods scattered everywhere, it really is an amazing place. At night especially, it feels like you've been transported to a magical environment.

Marty settled in quickly and soaked up the warmth and peace. With his days at Sky clearly numbered, he decided to write a business plan for a new venture he was keen to set up. It would involve being a consultant: drawing on his skills and experience to provide a service in the areas of mentoring, coming up with creative ideas and working in the media. He also worked on his book *Raw*, a follow-up to the first autobiography he had released back in 1995.

Our days fell into a routine. We'd start with an early morning walk on the beach, followed by a swim, then head back to our private villa for breakfast. Marty would write for a couple of hours, while I read by the pool or went shopping. We'd have lunch together then spend the afternoon chilling.

The day would finish with dinner at one of the local restaurants. Our favourite was a place in Seminyak called Chandi: it served an Asian degustation menu that was to die for, and featured the most divine dessert ever, 'Hot Dark Chocolate Fondant with Organic Vanilla Bean Ice Cream'. It was so good we went back several nights in a row.

The holiday was wonderful, and I remember thinking how blessed I was to have this beautiful man who loved romance and travel, and made me so very happy.

Marty and me on our blissful holiday in Bali in 2012.

We got home on 7 October, feeling refreshed and invigorated. Marty was excited about working on his new business venture. But before he could throw himself into it, he had a couple of things to get out of the way, including an appointment with a head and neck specialist.

Before we went to Bali, Marty had noticed some swollen glands in his neck and had gone to see our doctor, Anna Twhigg. She did a needle biopsy, and the results showed that he had a mild infection. But Anna wanted to be sure, so as a precaution she advised him to see a specialist for a second opinion.

Marty went to see Mark Izzard as soon as we got back from Bali, and was asked to make a booking for a CT scan. The day after the scan, I returned home from running some errands to find Marty standing at the kitchen counter, staring at his iPad. When he turned around, I saw that he was crying. He didn't say a word; he just handed me his iPad.

I looked at what he had been googling and two words jumped out at me: 'lymphoma' and 'cancer'.

Chapter Fifteen

Marty had been driving Emma to a tennis lesson when Mark Izzard called with the scan results. The phone was on speaker, so Emma, then nine, heard Mark tell her father what was wrong.

'Papa, what's lymphoma?' she asked. Marty was relieved that Mark hadn't used the word cancer.

After dropping Emma off, Marty raced home to google lymphoma; he was still trying to process the information when I arrived. My heart stopped for a moment when I saw those words on his iPad. Then we fell into one another's arms, crying.

Jasmine walked in a moment later and asked what was happening. I told her about Marty's diagnosis in very simple terms, then took her downstairs to her room—I sensed Marty needed to be alone.

I needed a moment myself to absorb the shocking news. When the word 'cancer' is mentioned, you immediately think the worst—that it could be a death sentence. My dear friend Jean had died of cancer in May that year, and I was still mourning her loss. Plus there was the cancer scare I had recently been through with Mum.

I kept thinking, *How can this be happening to my beautiful soulmate?* I was overwhelmed with fear, but somehow I went onto autopilot and set about supporting Marty and doing what needed to be done. I rang his mother Audrey and his sister Deb to break the news, while Marty rang Emma's mum Huhaana.

That night we read everything we could about lymphoma on the internet, although we didn't know at that stage what sort

Marty and I had a deep and soulful connection that helped us through the tough times.

Marty had. It was very confronting and scary. My advice to new patients now would be to refrain from reading anything until you know exactly what your diagnosis is.

One thing I did notice was that lymphoma affects the immune system, and that didn't surprise me. Over the years Marty had often had poor immunity. Just about every time he went on a plane, he ended up with a cold. Night sweats are another symptom of lymphoma, and he'd been experiencing those for the last few months.

The following day, Marty had a biopsy to establish the extent of the cancer. He learned that he had follicular lymphoma, a slow-growing indolent blood disease that was present throughout his lymphatic system. It was incurable, but the symptoms could be treated and the disease managed for many years. According to some material we read, people with this condition live for an average of seven years, or have a sixty percent chance of remission. Other sources said you could live well with the disease for many years—sometimes without needing treatment—because of its slow-growing nature. We had to hope that this was going to be the case for Marty.

After breaking the awful news to our families and closest friends, we knew we would have to put a press statement out. It was best for the truth to be known, rather than to have people speculating when they heard Marty was ill. We would also be able to ask for privacy, so we could get on with doing what needed to be done.

I use the word 'we' deliberately, because from the moment I found out Marty had cancer, it was my diagnosis as well. I knew I was going to walk every step of this journey with him. He was the love of my life, and I was the love of his; we had to do this together.

Marty needed me more than ever, and he would often tell people how strong I was. I was only strong because I had to be. For me to be of any help to Marty, I had to remain calm, especially when his fear threatened to overwhelm him. There were a lot of decisions to make about his treatment, and I was there with him at every appointment, listening to what was being said and helping him understand all the information. But it was Marty who made all the final decisions on what he wanted to do.

While I was being Marty's support, I had my own team of dear friends backing me up. There's a saying that goes, 'Behind every good man is a good woman'. I would add that behind every good woman is her support team. Those few precious people kept me going, and I knew I could rely on them to be there for me whenever I needed them.

I also had support from two trusted clairvoyants at different stages of Marty's cancer journey. They kept me grounded, knowing I was protected by loving energy whenever the dark times came.

Marty's close friend Dave Morris became a pillar of strength for both of us. Dave's wife also suffered from lymphoma, so he had a deep understanding of what the disease involved. He and Marty had a long history together, going back to their days at Auckland Grammar, and as Marty's journey progressed Dave walked the whole distance with us.

Dave has a strong faith, as does my friend Patricia, who was my rock. That faith we all shared was my constant refuge. When I thought I couldn't keep going, it helped me put one foot in front of the other.

The day after we publicly announced that Marty had lymphoma, I was booked to do a live twenty-minute TV segment on The Shopping Channel for Living Nature. I could have pulled out given the circumstances, but the company had worked so hard to get the spot. As the main spokesperson for the brand, I felt that I really needed to do it.

And so I prayed, asking God to help me through it. My prayers were answered when the presenter working with me turned out to be the lovely Lucy Gallaugher. We connected instantly, and that made it so much easier to get through that very long twenty minutes. I held it together until I climbed into the car with Lou Henderson to leave, and then I burst into tears. I couldn't be brave for a moment longer.

When you're dealing with a diagnosis of cancer, one of the things you have to cope with is the reaction from other people. We learned so much from what we went through that I'd like to offer a personal insight into what helped and what didn't. Bear in mind that the person who has just been diagnosed—and their loved ones—will be working through a vast body of information, trying to make decisions about treatment and how to proceed. Marty was doing his own research, reading up about treatments and lifestyle changes, but he was also bombarded by well-meaning people offering their advice. Both he and I would get lengthy emails full of details about different cancer treatments, but often they were too overwhelming to even try to read.

Based on our experience, my advice would be to ask first if the person would like to hear what you have to share with them—this puts the ball in their court. It's important to remember that you can't know what someone is going through at every stage of their journey, and as well intentioned as your assistance might be, it could be too much for them to cope with at that particular time.

According to everything we read, there was no obvious cause for follicular lymphoma. But Marty was adamant that he knew why he'd got it. He believed that the emotional stress he'd been under for many years—and the stress he was currently going through with his job—played a part in him developing cancer.

Thanks to being such a good cricket player, Marty had been thrust into the limelight at a young age, and he missed out on a lot of the normal emotional development a teenage boy should go through. When life threw him challenges he didn't always know how to deal with them, and at times he reacted in ways that weren't good for him or anyone else involved. He would suppress his emotions and then hold on to them, instead of releasing them and moving on. He would go over and over what had happened in his mind until it festered there, causing even more stress.

He wrote in his diary, 'Mr Cancer was a result of me constantly feeding the unweeded garden a toxic poison of deep-rooted negative thoughts. Cancer forced me to make a choice—deal with the weeds and watch the two roses in my life [Lorraine and Emma] blossom, or lie down and die.'

Marty identified with what Louise Hay had written about cancer in her bestselling book, *You Can Heal Your Life*: that the disease was a result of deep hurt, long-standing resentment and carrying hatreds. Marty believed all of that was true for him.

He knew he had to do some serious work on his mind if he had any chance of beating the cancer—or the 'snake in the grass', as he called it. That snake might be lying still for now, but it could make its move at any time if Marty let his emotional guard down.

One of the first things Marty did after his diagnosis was begin counselling sessions with Diana Newcomb, known as Didi. A cancer survivor, Didi had written a book called *Cancer: Don't Buy Its Terror Tactics*. She believed that her cancer had been brought on by her emotions, and when Marty read that, it resonated with him instantly. His sessions with Didi unleashed a whole barrage of deep-seated emotions he'd been hanging on to. I would wake up some nights to hear the sound of sobbing coming from downstairs, and I'd find Marty lying on the floor, the emotion pouring out of him.

I'd watch quietly until he'd finished releasing everything, then I'd go to him and hold him. His body would feel relaxed and calm in my arms, and I knew that this process of letting go was good for him.

Didi was a godsend. She was able to connect with Marty and guide him—sometimes gently, sometimes not so gently—so that he could understand the destructive thinking that had become a habit after so many years of practice. She showed him his ego and how it could make him fearful.

She also showed him how to shut down that ego when the fearful thoughts came, and to say to the constant questioning voice in his head, 'I don't care.'

Doing this was a huge challenge for Marty—his negative thinking had dominated his psyche for thirty years. But he now believed that those thought patterns had caused his cancer, and accepted that he needed to change. Didi taught Marty about meditating, which was the ideal tool for him as it required him to still his mind. It was a technique he could turn to when the suffering became too much.

These counselling sessions helped him to find inner peace. As he wrote in his autobiography *Raw*: 'Everything around me started to appear differently. I saw things in people, in nature, in life in general that generated love and goodwill, compassion and understanding, laughter and joy, peace, harmony and tranquillity. I even saw it in myself.'

It was so good for me to see that Marty had finally found self-love. He had always been his own biggest critic, and a very harsh critic at that. Deep down he had disliked himself very much, and that broke my heart. We all loved him for the kind-hearted, generous and gentle man that he was; why couldn't he love himself too? Dave Morris touched on this when he wrote a beautiful song for Marty called 'You are Loved'.

So, as hideous as it was that Marty had cancer, it was taking him down a much-needed path of spiritual healing, and that was very enlightening for him.

In those first six weeks after diagnosis, Marty made some massive changes. Apart from the counselling sessions with Didi, he altered his diet, took supplements, drank disgusting-tasting concoctions, had intravenous vitamin C and K to boost his immune system, and even underwent colonic irrigation.

When he went for tests at six weeks the results were a huge relief: the 'snake' was lying still and there was no sign of it in his bone marrow. He was given 'wait and watch' status, which meant he didn't need any medical treatment for the time being.

'Whatever you've been doing, keep doing it, and come back and see me in three months,' his haematologist said.

But in the weeks that followed, Marty had to deal with a stressful and upsetting situation involving a close cricketing friend who was being badly treated. Marty was so angry that his emotions went into overdrive, undoing some of the progress he'd made with Didi. I watched this unfold, knowing it wasn't going to be good for him.

And sure enough, just three weeks after that appointment, he developed an intense pain in his stomach. It was so bad that I drove him to Auckland Hospital, where the staff decided to check him in under the name 'Vincent Brightside' to give him some privacy. The funny part was that they didn't tell me about their plan, so when I returned to the hospital after racing home to get a few things, I had no idea which ward he was on until I discovered his new identity.

> 'He knew he had to urgently distance himself from the politics of cricket and the media, and focus on his spiritual and physical wellbeing. It was no longer a case of 'wait and watch'—Marty needed immediate chemotherapy to reduce the tumour.'

At least we could have a bit of a laugh over that while the doctors ran tests to find out what was causing Marty's stomach pain. Unfortunately, the result of the tests was no laughing matter. There was a new growth in Marty's abdomen.

He was convinced that this growth had appeared as a result of the stress he'd been under in the past three weeks, because he'd allowed himself to be drawn into the unjust situation affecting his friend.

He knew he had to urgently distance himself from the politics of cricket and the media, and focus on his spiritual and physical wellbeing.

It was no longer a case of 'wait and watch'—Marty needed immediate chemotherapy to reduce the tumour, which was causing a lot of pain. Fear raged through him, and I was grateful that I had Didi to help me calm him.

There was a lot more work to be done for my beautiful man. Perhaps the author Eckhart Tolle said it best when he wrote: 'For most people, their spiritual teacher is their suffering. Because eventually the suffering brings about awakening.'

On 24 January 2013, Marty and I arrived at Mercy Hospital where he was to begin the first of six chemotherapy sessions; these would be spread out over the following six months. As we reached the door, Marty halted, then fell into my arms like a scared child.

I held him for a few moments.

'We will be fine, and we'll get through this, but you have to accept it and rise above it,' I said. I smiled at him and he nodded, and we went in.

Chemotherapy is brutal. People react differently to it, and while some can be back at work the next day, others have a more severe reaction. Marty was in that second group. Chemo really hit him hard.

More than once he had a reaction to the drugs, and the staff had to stop administering them and give him other drugs to combat the reaction; then the chemo would be resumed. It was frightening to watch the first time this happened, but the nursing staff were amazing and got everything under control.

I sat with Marty for each of his chemo sessions and they were very long days. Sometimes we'd be there for nine hours. After the chemo Marty would go through ten days of really hard times. He'd have a nasty metallic taste in his mouth, constant nausea and sometimes vomiting, constipation from all the pills, and zero energy. The lack of energy was particularly upsetting for him because he felt like he was letting me and Emma down—which of course he wasn't. He lost his voice, too, and at times it was little more than a squeak.

But the worst thing was the tinnitus: a constant high-pitched ringing in the ears, which Marty described as the crashing sound of cicadas. It seemed to be connected to his heartbeat, and there was no relief from it. The tinnitus actually started the day after he was diagnosed, and he couldn't get a break from the relentless buzzing in his ears.

'Raine, this is worse than the chemo,' he told me.

It never went away, but he learned to live with it.

During chemo Marty lost all of his hair, including his eyebrows and eyelashes. He stopped wearing the hairpiece he had worn for the last twenty years, which pleased me because I had never liked it. The only reason he wore it for all that time was that he was contracted to do it, so having it on paid some bills. Not needing to wear it anymore was actually liberating: the hairpiece wasn't true to the person he really was.

> 'Chemotherapy is brutal. People react differently to it, and while some can be back at work the next day, others have a more severe reaction. Marty was in that second group. Chemo really hit him hard.'

On the eleventh day after chemo he would start to feel better. He'd be able to resume meditating, doing a little bit of exercise and going to counselling. His sessions with Didi now were about forgiveness—forgiving himself and other people—and I saw a more peaceful Marty emerging.

After day 11 we could go for our beloved walks together, and Emma was able to come and stay. Emma was the best tonic for Marty—she gave him pure, unconditional love, and was one of the reasons he was so determined to live.

The kindness of my friends helped me immensely during this time. My caring and thoughtful friend Frances sent bouquets of flowers every month, and others would bring food to put in

Frances Jones has been a wonderful friend to Marty and me.

our freezer. The lovely Patricia dropped off delicious chicken vegetable soup and stewed pears every week. Being a caregiver for someone going through chemo is exhausting, and knowing there was a meal ready to go was a godsend for me.

Marty's treatment finally finished in June, and we waited for the scan results to see what had happened to the tumour. He slowly started regaining energy, and we gained a little of our life back. We made a conscious decision to find something every day that brought us joy. It could be looking at a sunrise or sunset, listening to Jasmine tell us a funny story, watching Em doing her gymnastics or Dave playing his guitar (he would come over when Marty was unable to do anything but lie still, and play and sing to him for an hour or two).

It didn't matter how bad Marty felt or how awful the day was, we always found joy in something. Otherwise life would have been too bleak.

The scan results, when they came, were good: the chemo appeared to have done its job and reduced the previously enlarged lymph nodes in his abdomen to around 1.5 cm, indicating a very good response to treatment. Marty was told that he would remain under observation for the next five years, but he could take a break from treatment as long as the cancer didn't start to grow again. That was something to be very joyous about!

He now had to focus on staying as well as possible, while I tried to get on with normal life again.

Chapter Sixteen

When Marty was going through chemo, I was fortunate to be able to drop some of my commitments to concentrate on being there for him. But daily life had to go on, and it was time to continue my image consulting work. I also needed to be there for other members of my family, particularly my daughter, Jasmine.

At sixteen, Jasmine was more passionate than ever about dancing and knew that she wanted to make it her career. My role was to help her achieve her dream, which meant helping out wherever needed. On any given day I was her personal assistant, taxi driver, chef, wardrobe mistress, and/or hair and make-up artist at competitions. It required sacrifice in some respects, but it was worth it because she loved to dance so much.

In January 2014, six months after Marty's chemo ended, I took Jasmine to a week-long dance workshop at Dance World, a performing arts school in Melbourne. She loved every minute, and gained a huge amount from the experience. On the last day we were asked to meet with Dance World's artistic director, Pamela Apostolidis, and head of administration, Hayley Russell. They were so impressed with Jasmine that they offered her a scholarship for their two-year dance diploma.

We were both over the moon, but I was unsure about the timing.

'Since she's only sixteen and needs to finish her education in New Zealand, would it be possible to defer your offer for a couple of years?' I asked.

Pamela's reply was an adamant 'No'. They wanted to start working with her immediately—mainly for technical reasons to do with her dance development.

So we came home with a very important decision to make. Jasmine, of course, desperately wanted to go because it was an incredible opportunity, and in my heart I knew that we would be crazy to turn it down. After lengthy discussions with her father and Marty, we accepted the scholarship offer.

I had one condition: the school had to find a family for Jasmine to live with, as I did not want her flatting at the age of sixteen. We also agreed that she would finish her school studies via correspondence, which she did (after a long day of dancing she would go home and study, which required great discipline. I'm very proud of my daughter).

We had just a week after making the decision to get her back to Melbourne for the start of term one. It was a week of utter craziness. One particularly mad moment sticks in my mind. Jasmine had just got a new passport, and I was sitting at the kitchen bench, reading about how you should clip the corner off the old one so you could tell it had expired. I grabbed the scissors and diligently snipped off a corner of her passport—only to realise that instead of cutting hers, I'd just cut my own current one!

The language that came out of my mouth gave me a fright! It was one of those moments when you know you have stuffed up and there's nothing you can do about it.

I did try gluing the corner back on but I knew it was a bad idea—I couldn't risk being turned away at immigration as I really needed to go to Melbourne with Jasmine to get her settled in. The next day saw me frantically organising a new passport, parting with a scary amount of money to ensure it arrived before we flew out.

Marty dropped us at the airport safely on departure day, but half an hour later he received a call from me: I had left an important folder of documentation at home. Back he came with the folder, getting there in the nick of time before we had to board . . . and then we discovered that Jasmine had left her passport on the table in the airport café!

She was lucky to get it back, and I was a complete mess by the time we finally collapsed into our seats on the plane. Jasmine and I looked at one another and we laughed and laughed.

Before we flew to Australia we had skyped the family Jasmine would be living with, and they seemed like lovely people. I spent the first night at their home in Melbourne with Jasmine, but after that I arranged alternative accommodation for myself. I wanted Jasmine to get used to being alone with the family, while knowing I was still nearby if she needed me.

As I watched her in the kitchen with the family one night, laughing and joking, I felt relieved but sad. But it wasn't until the next day, when I was in the city shopping for some last-minute items for Jasmine's room, that the reality hit me. I was losing my daughter, and I had allowed that to happen. The emotion of it gripped my whole being, and I was filled with gut-wrenching pain. My mind raced with thoughts: *I don't want to let her go; I want to take her home; why did I say yes to this?*

I realised in that moment what was happening—I'd been so busy organising everything and getting carried along in the excitement, I hadn't really processed it.

I retreated into a doorway and bawled my eyes out. It was several minutes before I could pull myself together enough to keep moving. I wandered around the city in a daze, now with a single thought running through my mind: *What have I done?*

Eventually it sunk in that what I had done was allow my daughter to pursue her dream. With that had come the inevitable moment of letting go. It was just that in my case, I'd had to do it much sooner than expected.

On the plane back to Auckland the next day, I reflected once again on one of my favourite books, *The Prophet* by Kahlil Gibran. It's a collection of poetic essays that are philosophical, spiritual and inspirational. One essay in that book that I particularly love is titled 'On Children', and it includes the line, 'You are the bows from which your children as living arrows are sent forth.'

I had just shot Jasmine off on her life journey, and I had to be strong.

I never let on to her how I was feeling—how could I? She was happy and excited about what lay ahead for her, and I didn't want her to worry about how much it was upsetting me.

Jasmine not only completed her school studies, but she also excelled at Dance World, receiving two dance diplomas and being named the Dance Department Dux for 2015. She's still in Melbourne pursuing her dance career, and she loves it so much that it's now her home for the foreseeable future. Thank God for technology, which means we can communicate every day. We are still as close as ever, and I am truly glad that she is living her dream and being so successful. She is happy with her life, and that makes me happy.

When I got back from Melbourne, not having Jasmine in the house took a bit of getting used to. Marty was doing well—he'd stayed with his family while I was away and had been able to spend quality time with them. The work he had been doing with Didi helped a lot when it came to undertaking emotional healing with his family. That was one of the lovely things that this hideous cancer led to: he was able to sort out past hurts and misunderstandings and draw closer to people. And for that, Marty was grateful.

I was feeling restless, and decided to do something radical. For about a year, I'd been talking to my hairdresser, Gareth Chitty, about cutting my hair short. Finally I said to him, 'Let's do it.'

They say that when a woman decides to chop her hair off, there is usually something emotional going on in her life. That was definitely the case for me!

I had actually had super-short hair once before, when I was thirty, but that was out of necessity. I'd asked my hairdresser for the fully bleached 'Loni Anderson' look the day before my thirtieth birthday. When I opened the door to my guests at my birthday

A modelling shot from the mid-1990s, when I first cut my hair short. Photo by Neil Gussey.

party and none of them acknowledged the very obvious change to my hair, I knew it was bad. I went back to my Wellington hairdresser, Clark York, the next day. He said we could try to reverse the colour, but I would probably lose a lot of hair.

'Or else you could keep the colour and go super short,' he suggested.

So that's what we did and it worked. I kept it short and enjoyed the cut for a year before growing it out again.

When I started thinking about going short again in 2014, my hair was probably looking the best it had ever been, but I was bored with it and needed a change. I know that sounds ungrateful, but between Marty's illness and Jasmine leaving home, I was feeling quite blue. I needed something to pick me up.

I had been admiring actress Charlize Theron's short haircut, which was sexy and still very feminine. We both have a natural wave, so I thought her cut could work on my hair. But I was very nervous when the big day rolled around, and eagerly accepted a glass of wine from Gareth when he offered it.

Having all my hair cut off was very liberating. It actually made me feel stronger, which I needed. Marty loved it—in fact when I decided to grow it back after eighteen months, he didn't want me to.

Some people thought it looked great and others didn't. Emma was very honest the first time she saw my new look.

'Raine, how long will it take to grow it back?' she asked.

I liked it—in fact I felt fantastic. My fiftieth birthday was looming in June, so it seemed right to be sporting a new look as I entered a new decade.

I wasn't fazed about turning fifty—age is just a number, and celebrating it meant that I got to spend time with some of my nearest and dearest.

The day before my birthday three of my closest friends—my earth angels, actually—flew up from Wellington and took me on a girls' road trip to Takahoa in the Kaipara for the night. Frances is a writer who co-wrote a book with me in 1998 (*REAL: The*

Top A surprise appearance by actress Teuila Blakely at my fiftieth birthday luncheon.

Above The gorgeous Katherine Beauchamp from Wellington was one of the friends who travelled to Auckland to celebrate my birthday with me.

Truth about Fashion, Beauty and Image); Kath started out as my office junior at Care of Lorraine and became a good friend; and Deborah was one of my models, whose loyalty and support when others left my agency has never been forgotten.

We had a fabulous night together, then came back to Auckland the next day for my birthday luncheon. My mum was there with my sisters—apart from Jenny, who skyped us from Dallas—and many other friends, including Sandra Allan, Julie Shearer, Liz Hicks, my schoolmate Patricia and Lou Henderson.

Patricia, who owned a café at the time, did the catering for the lunch and wowed us with her amazing food. Marty was our waiter and kept the champagne flowing. All my gorgeous gals shared their memories of times we'd spent together, and I felt quite overwhelmed with love—what more could a girl want?

But wait, there was more. My darling husband had arranged for a special guest to turn up: *Shortland Street* actress Teuila Blakely. At the time I was a big *Shortland Street* fan, and I had met Teuila once at a fundraising function and really enjoyed her company.

It was a huge surprise to have Teuila at my party, and Marty was delighted that he had been able to organise it. He was so thoughtful like that.

The following day, Marty and I flew to Queenstown to continue my birthday festivities in another stunning part of the country. I was a very lucky lady: my celebrations just went on and on, and every event was filled with love and laughter. It was wonderful to have such good times in the midst of what had been a difficult period.

Chapter Seventeen

The saying that you find out who your real friends are when you're down and out is true. My friends were all there for me on joyous occasions such as my fiftieth birthday, but more importantly, they were there when times got tough, especially when Marty was sick.

I don't have a huge group of friends, but the ones I do have are loyal and supportive, and I would be lost without them. I know I can pick up the phone at any time and my friends will be there for me, and that has been such a comfort, especially in the last few years.

Many years ago, Frances gave me a decorative box with an inscription on top that read, 'There's nothing more precious than a loyal friend. If you find one, cherish them.'

I have always treasured that gift, and treasured Frances. I cherish all of my friends—they really are crucial to my wellbeing.

When it comes to my general health and state of mind, I have tried a range of therapies, treatments and strategies over the years that have been helpful. I turned to many of these when Marty was sick, as well as in other tough times throughout my life. While I trust (and use) Western medicine, I also have an appreciation for the healing powers of holistic medicine, and I like the way it considers the whole person—mind, body and spirit.

I'd like to share some of the therapies and the people who've helped me in various ways: physically, mentally and emotionally.

We see professionals when there is something wrong with our bodies, so why shouldn't we see one who can treat our minds? Therapy can be very helpful at times in our lives when we feel lost, alone, sad or angry, or when we just need help understanding what is going on for us. I see people who are struggling and I often think, *Oh, if only you would go to see a professional to talk about this.* Yes, it takes courage to face up to your truth, but the reward you get—peace of mind—is so worth it.

When I was feeling depressed and lonely during the course of my first marriage, I went to see a psychologist in Wellington named Kay Allen. She was magnificent, helping me to understand who I was and how I had come to this point in my life. It is easy to lose our way at times, and a skilled practitioner who understands how our minds work can guide us back onto the path towards happiness and inner peace.

Murray and I also had counselling sessions with Kay. If your relationship is struggling, I think it's definitely worth seeking out a neutral third party who can help you talk through your issues. Twenty years on, I still have a chat with Kay when I feel it's needed.

When people tell me they don't like massages, I look at them as if they are crazy. I love this kind of therapy and I always feel so good afterwards. Shiatsu helped me enormously after the break-up of my first marriage. My Wellington therapist, Susan, was so gentle with me at a time when I needed support.

Shiatsu stimulates the body's vital energy, known as *qi* or *ki*. Susan would ask me to 'breathe into' different parts of my body (heart, kidneys, stomach). At times I found this hugely affecting; on one occasion I started sobbing without any warning. I knew that a deep healing was taking place as my body released lots of emotions I'd been holding on to.

My therapist in Auckland, Amy, offers a relaxing Thai massage with hot rocks, which is great for releasing those tight knots you get from holding tension in your body. I tend to judge a treatment by how I feel when I leave, and after Amy has worked her magic I always feel 'out of it' in a blissful way and have to concentrate hard on driving home.

I go to see clairvoyants because I do believe there are people in this world who've been gifted—by a higher power—with the ability to connect with those who have passed over into the spirit world. Through these special people, our loved ones can give us messages from the other side to help us along our path or give us clarity about what is happening in our lives.

I've visited quite a few clairvoyants over the years and it has always been a positive experience for me. Two ladies in particular have had quite an impact. One was Kay Hewson in Wellington, the first clairvoyant I ever saw. She's the person I mentioned earlier who passed on messages from my dad.

Kay also told me that 'they' (the people who were coming through in spirit) had a message for me about my son: he should turn down the volume on his headphones because the loud music was damaging his hearing. After that session I took Hilton to have his hearing checked, and there were indeed signs of early hearing loss. I believe Kay now lives in Ashhurst.

The second clairvoyant to make a big mark was Angel Andrea, whom I started seeing just before Marty first fell ill. Andrea walked with me along the path of Marty's illness and beyond, and I felt her loss deeply when she passed away in July 2017. I will be forever grateful to Andrea for her love, her advice and her amazing hugs. When Andrea wrapped you in her arms, you never wanted her to let go. Her eyes were full of the deepest love I have ever seen. Arohanui, Andrea.

When I arrived in Auckland in 2007 sporting that huge haematoma on my forehead, my doctor referred me to a physiotherapist, the lovely Susan Lugton. As she treated my injury, Susan noticed that my breathing was shallow. She tried to teach me a technique for breathing properly through the nose, drawing the breath up from the diaphragm. But I couldn't get the hang of it; there was a lot going on in my mind at the time.

Susan continued to treat me for some back issues I was having, and after a while she had another go at teaching me how to breathe properly. This time something clicked and I was able to master the technique.

Proper deep breathing can calm the mind and reduce stress, and has benefits for the whole body. If you want to learn to meditate, understanding how to breathe properly is a good place to start—focusing on your breath takes you away from your thoughts, making it easier to meditate successfully.

I took Jasmine to see Susan for a couple of breathing sessions when she was getting anxious before her dancing competitions, and the skills Susan taught her were invaluable.

During Marty's illness I would wake regularly in the night, filled with anxiety about what the future held for him and for us. I found that if I practised Susan's breathing exercises, I was usually able to settle back to sleep.

Yoga is another wonderful way of calming the mind. I first tried it not long after my first marriage ended, when a dear friend, Mel McGoldrick, invited me to a class run by Philip Savage at Yoga Space in Wellington. After ninety minutes, I floated out of the room on a cloud, and it occurred to me that I hadn't once thought about the problems I'd been dealing with. Yoga had shut down the incessant chattering in my brain.

Yoga is great not only for quieting the mind, but also for healing the body: it massages you internally, getting your blood flowing. I have never left a yoga class without feeling blissed out and amazing. I always think of yoga as nourishing my mind, body and soul.

Susan, my physio, recommended classes in Auckland taken by Karla Brodie, who has since become my yoga angel. Karla is incredible—she has a gift for knowing what people need from her classes, and she can tell just by looking at me if my neck is tight or my back is sore.

The yoga Karla teaches is not just about holding poses or positions; it's an approach to being. It's about moving with ease and grace, always in harmony with the day, the weather, the season and whatever's happening in your life. Karla encourages you to listen to how your body is feeling. If you need to adjust a pose to feel more comfortable, you can. What matters is what works for you.

My all-time favourite form of yoga is called restorative yoga: this is where you get wrapped up in blankets and you drift off into a deep state of relaxation. It's just heavenly, and I've been working on building the techniques into my routine at home. Restorative yoga is a great way of gently waking the body and reconnecting with yourself and with God (or whatever higher power you believe in).

Through studying yoga, I've picked up lots of things I can do for my wellbeing—something as simple as lying with my feet up the wall for ten minutes can make me feel more energised. Yoga is a practice I really want to keep up, especially now that I'm getting older. It is my gift to myself.

In 1995, while I was rehearsing to model in the Benson & Hedges Fashion Awards, I did something pretty serious to my lower back—it was so bad that I couldn't actually move. One of the other models, Janine Foy, arranged a reiki session for me with a friend of hers.

Reiki is a healing technique that involves a practitioner channelling energy into a patient through touch. The therapist lays their hands on the area needing work, and this activates natural healing processes in the body, restoring physical and emotional wellbeing. If you have a friend with a sore lower back, you can try these principles at home: sit behind the patient and gently place your hands on the affected area. Your friend will feel the heat that radiates from your touch, and this can help to ease their pain and increase their mobility.

I haven't had the opportunity to use reiki since, but the results in this instance were amazing: I went from being unable to move to getting back on the catwalk. I certainly wouldn't be afraid to try it again.

These days, if I need serious bodywork done I see an osteopath, the very gifted Jeremy King of Bodyworx. When you've put your back out after lifting something heavy, or if you are suffering from any pain, he is your go-to guy. Jeremy and his team work on a deeper level, similar to Karla Brodie.

Marty introduced me to his acupuncturist, Peter Caughey, after I moved back to Auckland in 2007. Peter had been treating Marty for years with great results, so when I found myself feeling a bit lethargic, we thought that Peter might be able to help.

I liked Peter's energy from the moment we met—he was kind, upbeat, and he smiled a lot. I'd never had acupuncture before and I was nervous about having needles poked into me, but Peter was gentle and the needles he used were very fine, so it didn't hurt.

Unfortunately, that wasn't the case with the acupuncturist I saw after Peter moved to Bali. I found it very painful when she administered the needles, and I gave up after a few sessions; it just hurt too much and I dreaded going. Choosing the right practitioner is obviously paramount.

One of the treatments Peter used was moxibustion, which involves burning the herb mugwort in a small cone attached to the needle. This helps with deeper healing but, unfortunately, the smoke does smell a bit like marijuana. If you have to go back to the office afterwards, be aware that your clothes might give off this odour!

I still have acupuncture with Peter when he comes back to New Zealand, and he is an amazing man whose treatments touch clients on a deeper level. I look forward to the chats we have during our sessions—I always receive an abundance of wisdom from him.

In Peter's words, his mission is to support people to 'break free from limiting belief stories that stop them from living their true potential as a human being', and his gift as a healer and teacher is to help clients 'discover the true essence of who they are and live their life with abundant freedom'.

I love this, and I totally believe in it.

Among the other things that have saved me and kept me sane over the years is aromatherapy. I have been using oils since I was in my twenties, and my children have grown up with aromatherapy oils and candles in our home. I have an acute sense of smell (which is a hindrance sometimes) and I've found that different oils really do have an impact on how I feel.

There are many ways to use oils and reap their benefits. I found that a couple of drops of lavender in the bath helped to calm my kids down before bed. And I used tea tree and lemon oil in Hilton's rugby boots and Jasmine's ballet shoes to get rid of the pong! With my image consulting clients, I often burned orange and rosemary oils for their uplifting and positive effects. Eucalyptus is great for fighting colds, especially when added to a diffuser in the bedroom at night, when breathing can be congested. I have introduced oils into my household products as well.

As with anything, the quality of an oil affects its results—I always look for certified products so that I know I can trust what I'm getting.

Music is something else that is vital to my wellbeing. It can transport me back in time and remind me of a person or place; it can make me feel happy, sad, energised or melancholy. I play music every day. I'll choose something upbeat such as Michael Jackson when I need plenty of energy, and something more mellow in the evening when I am winding down—maybe some George Michael. My children are music lovers too, and I'm convinced Jasmine's love of dance began in the womb when she could hear what I was playing. I've got some classic video clips of Hilton dancing to Bill Haley's rendition of 'Rock Around the Clock' when he was about two.

Driving to music makes me feel free. Whitney Houston and Adele, in particular, move my soul and take me to a place of deep gratitude, where I feel thankful to be alive.

Similarly, I can't imagine my life without dancing. I've already shared my passion for the Argentinian tango, but I'm also a big fan of eighties music and of soul artists such as Stevie Wonder and Earth, Wind & Fire. I love to get up and have a boogie. It doesn't matter if you can't dance—just do it like nobody is watching!

One of the things I have found most helpful also happens to be completely free, and anyone can enjoy it. I'm talking about nature, God's greatest gift to the human race. When I'm feeling out of sorts, going for a walk along the beach or through the bush can make me feel like a new person. The sun is a great source of healing, and even being caught in a rain shower can be glorious, leaving you invigorated. Watching sunrises and sunsets makes my soul feel alive. If everything is getting too much, go out and just enjoy nature if you can—it will lift you immensely. Never underestimate the incredible power of nature.

NY
BULLS
1

Chapter Eighteen

Now that Marty was no longer having chemo and had a lot more energy, he was able to do some work mentoring young people. He found that process as enriching for him as it was for them. He also worked closely with two of his good friends, New Zealand cricketers Ross Taylor and Martin Guptill, in a mentoring role. Being able to pass on his deep understanding and knowledge of the game gave him enormous joy.

But in September 2014, shortly before his fifty-second birthday, we got some bad news. The deadly snake within him had started moving again. The tumour in his stomach was growing and the disease had changed from low-grade follicular lymphoma to an aggressive fast-growing form called B-cell lymphoma. Marty's haematologist said he needed chemotherapy—immediately. We were also warned that this chemotherapy (known as R-ICE) would be stronger than the first (R-CHOP).

While Marty was obviously disappointed, he'd had two years of counselling and was better prepared this time around for what he was about to face. Or so he thought.

Marty's first chemo session was booked for 22 September—his fifty-second birthday—so the day before, we had a small group of close friends and family over for a birthday luncheon. After we'd eaten, Dave Morris and another musically gifted friend, broadcaster Tim Roxborogh, brought out their guitars and the singing commenced. There was plenty of laughter, and tears too. If somebody wanted to cry, they could and it was totally okay. Our life had a raw honesty about it by then.

At the end of the luncheon Marty said to us all, 'Don't worry, I will be okay.' In fact, the next day was to be the start of one of the worst weeks of his life.

Marty's previous chemo sessions had been at the small private Mercy Hospital, where he was given his own room and didn't have to deal with being recognised. However, this time round, the chemo was administered in the oncology day-stay ward at Auckland Hospital, which was full of other patients.

Marty was okay with that, but a couple of hours into the treatment he started experiencing terrible pain in his lower back. He didn't want to disturb the other patients, but it got so severe that he couldn't help screaming. The staff there didn't seem to believe how bad it was, even though it said in his notes that he was sensitive to chemotherapy. One of them suggested that I go and get a coffee as Marty was 'playing up'.

I knew my husband, and I had never seen him in so much pain, yet they would only give him Panadol. In the end I did leave as suggested, and I sat in the car, sobbing and feeling utterly helpless. When I went back I hoped things might have changed, but he was still crying out in absolute agony.

The curtain had been closed around Marty's bed, but we both heard the words of the nurse who was administering chemo to the patient in the next bed.

'Oh, you are the model patient, you should be proud of yourself.'

It felt to us that the nurse intended us to overhear. Marty looked at me, and I could tell something serious was happening. This was not a case of 'playing up'.

The staff decided that Marty should have a scan, and we were taken up to the radiology department. Emergency cases had to be seen first, and as he was not considered an emergency we had to wait nearly two hours. He'd had no serious pain relief, so he was in unbearable distress. And we were on our own, with no nurses there to help.

Marty eventually had the scan at around 4 p.m., and afterwards he was taken back to the day-stay ward. He looked at me with dazed eyes.

'This has got me, Raine,' he said. 'I'm scared.'

At around 5 p.m. he lost it, collapsing off the bed in front of his haematologist. He was finally given morphine and admitted for the night so that his pain could be managed.

Marty was put in ward 63, the stroke ward, which was the only one with an available bed. The staff there were lovely. We felt safe at last, and I tried to sleep in a chair in the corner of the room.

But at 3 a.m. Marty was awake.

'Raine, I'm frozen; I can't move,' he said to me.

Because the problem was to do with his lower back, he called his osteopath, Simon Kelly, who came up to the hospital at 6 a.m. Simon found that Marty had a sacroiliac subluxation, which meant that the joint responsible for helping him to walk had locked up and was setting off all the pain nerves in the area. That explained why Marty was in such agony. Simon treated him and helped to ease his pain.

Marty was then moved to the brand-new $8 million Motutapu Ward for adult oncology patients. The criteria for admission is high, so you generally have to be very sick to be there. The ward is impressive, with private rooms and an extra bed for loved ones to stay over. By this stage I was feeling like a zombie from the stress of the previous day and the lack of sleep, so it was a relief to be able to get some rest.

Chemo was resumed and continued for the next five days, and it was hideous. Marty suffered from awful nausea and vomiting, along with a relentless migraine. To make matters worse, at one stage, the job of taking blood was given to a new nurse who had great difficulty getting the line in. She finally managed after quite a few attempts. It was painful to watch, so I hate to think what it must have been like for Marty.

I understand that all new nurses have to learn somehow, but

after the couple of days that he'd had—and the fact that he was not tolerating the chemo very well—I felt that it would have been better to have someone experienced perform the task. I mentioned this to a senior member of staff, who instantly replied, 'Of course.' She understood where I was coming from.

As a caregiver, there are times when you have to speak up on behalf of your loved one; you have to be their voice when they cannot use theirs. I learned that you should never be scared to discuss your concerns with medical staff. If something is troubling you, it's always better to get it out there than to stay quiet.

Fortunately, this incident was a rare event: ninety-five percent of our dealings with the team that treated Marty were wonderful. It just happened that things didn't go well that particular day.

After the toll that chemo had taken on Marty, we thought things couldn't get worse. We were wrong. On Thursday, 25 September, while Marty was still in Motutapu Ward, I got a call from his haematologist.

'I need to have a meeting with you and Marty, and it's important that Marty's not drugged up when I talk to you both,' he said.

I took a deep breath. Clearly, this was going to be a serious conversation, and something bad was coming.

When we met with the haematologist I felt sick. He told us that further testing showed the lymphoma had transformed yet again. It was no longer just B-cell lymphoma, but double hit lymphoma, a very rare and aggressive form of the disease. This development was akin to a 'turbo switch' being flipped, and meant we were dealing with a much faster-growing cancer.

We were told that not a lot was known about this type of lymphoma, but what they did know was that chemo might have no effect. For most patients, the prognosis is not good.

Marty and I were both very still as we absorbed the information. The haematologist left the room to allow us to process what he'd told us, and we held one another and cried until Marty fell asleep.

As Marty slept, I sat in the silence, alone and stunned. We had just been told that this cancer could take Marty's life much sooner than we'd thought. The whole situation was surreal.

'Dear God, please give me courage,' I prayed. Then I phoned family and friends to pass on the heartbreaking update. Their responses told me that they were just as shocked as I was. Somehow I found the strength to make those calls and answer people's questions. I felt as if I was being guided by a greater source.

As the partner of someone going through terrible times like this, you do what you can to be strong and get on with whatever needs to be done. During our stay on the Motutapu Ward, I would see the partners of other patients and recognise the look in their eyes. We all had it: the inner knowledge that we were part of a special 'club' none of us wanted to belong to. Every one of us was exhausted, trying to face the truth that we could lose our loved one at any stage.

The day after the brutal diagnosis, I talked to the haematologist again to make sure I clearly understood what he was telling us. He repeated how serious double hit lymphoma was, and told me that he wanted to put Marty on a three-month treatment plan. This would involve two more rounds of chemo, followed by a scan to see if the tumour had shrunk. If it had gone down by half, they would give him another round of chemo, then collect his blood stem cells so that 'good' white cells could be frozen. This would be followed by 'big gun' chemo designed to kill off as much lymphoma as possible, before the frozen stem cells were put back in to start growing his bone marrow cells again.

Because of the high risk of infection, Marty would have the treatment in Motutapu Ward. If he went through the entire three-month plan, he would be in hospital for a total of four weeks or more.

It was a lot of information to take in.

'Why this treatment plan?' I asked.

'This is the best option to keep Marty alive,' I was told. 'Lymphoma that transforms is the most dangerous type to have.'

I asked what had caused the lymphoma to change but the haematologist couldn't give me a reason; it just had.

'There's nothing Marty could have done to prevent this happening,' he said.

I headed back to Marty's room, my mind churning with thoughts of losing my husband. I was so scared that I could hardly bear to think about what I had just been told. I sat beside Marty's bed and held on to his hand for dear life.

He woke up, and the first words he said were not what I was expecting.

'Raine, Jesus just came to me in my dream.'

He then proceeded to tell me what he had seen.

'A male figure, youngish and unshaven, wearing a waistcoat and jeans, stood over me and moved his hands over my body. He was checking the damage and said he would be back soon. He was warm and friendly, and he told me to sleep and meditate. He told me to have no fear. "Breathe deep," he said, then he was gone.'

The dream had comforted Marty.

We discussed the treatment plan that the haematologist wanted him to try. But after a lot of soul-searching, Marty came to a decision.

'Raine, I don't want to do it,' he said. 'With those uncertain survival rates, why would I spend the next three months going through torture, plus more time in recovery, and be left with only a little time to live?

'I want to go home and be able to live some life with you and Emma. I'm going to meditate, and do this my way with natural remedies, supplements and diet changes.'

As he shared his resolution with me, I felt at peace—and I knew that meant he'd made the right call. If I'd felt uneasy I would have pushed for him to give the treatment a try, but the sense of calmness that washed over me was a sign that this was meant to be. As always, I believed in listening to my gut feeling.

Plus, at the end of the day, it had to be Marty's decision.

It was his life; his choice.

We packed up and left the Motutapu Ward. Marty had only been in there a few days, but it felt like a lifetime. He still had to get over the hideous side effects of his last chemo session. It was tough, and seeing him going through

Me and my beautiful friend
Patricia Adams glammed
up for my sister's wedding.

all the nausea and misery made it clear that his decision not to proceed any further had been for the best.

Marty had come to another decision. He didn't know how much longer he had left, and he wanted me to stop work so that we could be together around the clock. I was determined to do this for him. Fortunately he had income insurance, which meant that we could manage financially. If we hadn't had that, I don't know what we would have done.

By this stage working had become tricky anyway, because I was exhausted physically, emotionally and mentally. I was dealing with so many emotions about what was happening: not only mine and Marty's, but also the feelings of everyone else who loved and cared for him. We were all scared by this new diagnosis.

Thankfully, I had people around me like the lovely Patricia, who walked every step of this journey by my side. She sent me countless messages of support when I needed to hear them. Later, she told me that when she wrote those words, she felt as if she were being channelled by a greater source of love. I certainly believe she was.

Not long after the diagnosis of double hit lymphoma, I received one of Patricia's special messages.

'From somewhere you will be given the courage and strength to support Marty to live well in every day that he will have,' it read. 'You are his love and light, his power and his energy. You said that with your dad you wished you had the time before he passed; you have the time now, to make every day as positive as possible for Marty.

'I know you are emotionally and physically drained but find the warrior in you and keep pushing through each day. He needs you now more than he ever has. You can do it, because true love has no limits.'

And with those wise and loving words to guide me, I settled into making life as beautiful and peaceful as I could for Marty. That was my role now, and I would do it to the very best of my ability.

Chapter Nineteen

Just as he'd told his haematologist he would, Marty started researching natural remedies that might help with his lymphoma. His good mate, former All Black Grant Fox (affectionately known as Foxy), had used sea cucumber to treat his dog's lymphoma, so Marty gave sea cucumber a go.

One of the other substances Marty tried was something we couldn't talk about at the time, because it was illegal. But I have to say that cannabis oil made a huge difference to Marty's wellbeing. It was so beneficial for him that I feel it's something I need to speak out about now.

Just about every time Marty searched the internet for natural remedies to treat cancer, the words 'cannabis oil' popped up. Some of the material he read suggested that it could reduce the growth of tumours. The more he learned about its positive effects, the more interested he was in trying it. So he found a caring source he could purchase it from, and began using it daily.

It was crucial to respect the power of cannabis oil, and to get the dosage right. When he first started using it, Marty would stay in the bedroom until he felt he'd got the amount correct and could walk around the house safely. He had strict, self-imposed rules about the use of the oil: no running the bath or being near the fire, no visiting the kitchen or the pool, and definitely no driving. It was all basic common sense.

Possibly, we should have added 'no media interviews' to that list. He did once chat to a journalist after he'd taken cannabis oil, and once he started talking he didn't stop.

Other than that, he was very careful about using it. The oil cost a lot of money, but it was definitely worth it because it had so many benefits. The best thing was that it took his nausea away, which gave him his life back. No nausea meant he had an appetite again and could eat. He stopped losing weight and started consuming the nutrients he needed, and he looked really good.

With the nausea gone, he didn't have to take anti-nausea medication. One of the side effects of those drugs was incredibly painful constipation. So thanks to the cannabis oil, the constipation went, and so did the anti-constipation drugs.

He'd also been on drugs for anxiety, but he no longer needed those because the cannabis oil took away the frenzied fear about the future, leaving him relaxed and calm. I loved seeing him so peaceful and enjoying life again.

He was able to sleep and that was a godsend, especially with his tinnitus.

Seeing the effects of cannabis oil first-hand have made me a wholehearted supporter of its use for medicinal purposes. In December 2017, I was pleased to see the New Zealand government announce legislation giving terminally ill patients a legal defence for possession and use of medicinal cannabis. They also proposed a scheme that may eventually enable patients with a prescription to access these products at a pharmacy.

In December 2014, Marty had a scan that showed his tumour had shrunk by more than fifty percent, which was brilliant news. We both needed to relax, recharge and reflect, so we booked a trip to Aitutaki, a beautiful atoll in the Cook Islands. I hoped that the healing power of the sun would restore some of Marty's energy.

We headed off on what was meant to be a seven-day trip. Aitutaki was every bit as beautiful as we were expecting, but Marty's energy was up and down. Halfway through our stay, he had a very bad day that left him confined to bed. He seemed to be in a deep dream state and at times his body would thrash crazily from side to side, which was alarming for me to witness.

He was a lot better when he woke after four hours' sleep, so we went to the pool for a swim. He was getting in the water when he noticed a young girl there who reminded him of Emma. Thinking about his daughter, he was suddenly overwhelmed with emotion. He started sobbing, calling for me to help him from the pool.

'I need to write a letter to Emma,' he said, panicked, 'in case I don't see her again.'

The tears streamed down his face as he wrote Emma a 'Goodbye, my love' letter on his iPad.

We decided it would be best if we cut the holiday short and went home so that Marty could be close to Emma. Being away from her was troubling him too much. Air New Zealand were absolutely wonderful in making that possible for us—in fact there were several occasions when they helped us change our plans due to unforeseen circumstances. We felt very grateful.

When we got home, Marty resumed his intense counselling sessions with Didi, who encouraged him to work on healing his mind through meditation. By sitting still, he was able to reach a better understanding of his life, and of the part that the mind–body connection had played in him getting cancer.

He read voraciously, focusing on motivational authors such as Oriah, John Kehoe, Wayne Dyer, Osho, Stuart Wilde, Deepak Chopra, Eckhart Tolle, John Demartini, Sydney Banks and many more.

Through his reading and meditating, he gained a real purpose and a greater awareness of his authentic self. That judgemental 'ego' voice began to quieten, and he felt grounded and grateful.

Because of the hideous disease he received, Marty was changing into a peaceful man, whose true self emerged gracefully.

'I finally like who I am,' he told me.

Christmas 2014 was a big deal for us because we feared it could be Marty's last.

One day he would be fine; the next he'd be bedridden.

He never knew how he was going to feel from day to day. We just took each day as it came.

Marty's cousin Russell Crowe invited us to his farm near Coffs Harbour, Australia, for New Year's Eve. Emma and Jasmine went with us. We had quite a group: Marty's brother Jeff and his family, Russell's parents Alex and Jocelyn, Russell's sons Charlie and Tennyson and a bunch of Russell's friends, including some players from the rugby league team Russell owns: the South Sydney Rabbitohs.

The kids had a ball on Russell's property and it was a fun break from routine for us all. Marty coped well, so we started thinking about taking another family holiday while he was still strong enough to travel.

A little later, friends of Jeff's offered us the use of their house in Fiji for a week. Their Kiwi neighbours took us out for a day on the water in their launch, and we had a fantastic time. Emma took a photo of her beloved papa on the beach, looking strong and healthy.

But the next day, Marty came down with a cold and ended up very sick in bed. Once again we had to cut the trip short and go home, and once again Air New Zealand were very accommodating and offered exceptional service.

It was just so frustrating that one day Marty could be feeling great, and the day after he'd be really sick. We never knew what was coming next.

The 2015 Cricket World Cup was looming, to be jointly hosted by New Zealand and Australia. Marty had been the captain of the New Zealand cricket team the last time the cup was held here in 1992, and he was invited to promote the event and support the Black Caps.

He was being inundated with interview requests from the media, and had already committed to writing a weekly column for the website ESPNcricinfo.com as well as spending thirty days in Sydney, taking part in match coverage for ESPN. He was very excited about being involved in such a huge event, but he knew he

The family gathered together for Christmas 2014.

would have to be selective about what he did.

Naïvely, he agreed to do a press call at Eden Park early in January—his first interview since the return of his cancer had been announced back in September. Most of the questions were about his health, and he stood in the hot sun talking for quite some time. He arrived home a wreck, and told me he'd come very close to collapsing in front of the media. When I watched the interview on TV, I could see how much he was struggling.

Nobody, including the person who had arranged the press call, understood how ill and weak he really was. It took him a week in bed to recover.

After that interview, and others that followed, I found being out in public challenging. Well-meaning strangers would approach me in places like the supermarket to pass on their good wishes and even suggestions for treatment. I know they were being kind-hearted, but it was the last thing I needed at the time. I just wanted to get my groceries and go home.

Throughout the Cricket World Cup, Marty would put on a brave face and front up to different events, then come home and collapse. I worried about him, but he did enjoy being part of it. The highlight came on 28 February, during a pool match between New Zealand and Australia, when he was inducted into the International Cricket Council's Hall of Fame. It was a huge honour for Marty, and when he stepped out onto the ground at Eden Park in front of over 40,000 fans, the energy of the crowd was overwhelming. The cheering and clapping took his breath away—he could feel the love.

Marty gave a lovely acceptance speech, and I could see that he was happy to show his emotion—those days of holding it in were well and truly gone. He accepted the cap he was given in recognition of making it into the Hall of Fame, and gave it to his mum Audrey, thanking her for everything she had done for him. It was truly moving to see him honoured by the sport he had devoted so much to, and it gave him such a boost.

We flew to Sydney after that ceremony for the next few weeks of the World Cup. His cousin Russell was away overseas, but kindly lent us his home so that Marty would have somewhere private and comfortable to stay. It was far better than being based in a hotel room, and was close to where Marty was broadcasting for ESPN. Having the use of Russell's house made life much easier for Marty.

He was on a real high during that time, and his joy went through the roof when Martin Guptill turned in a quarter-final performance against the West Indies that Marty described as 'cricket heaven'. Marty had been mentoring Guppy and was delighted to see him do so well. When Guppy walked off at the end with a record score of 237 not out, Marty yelled out, 'Oh my Gup!' and popped open a bottle of bubbly. He marvelled for days over Guptill's performance.

> 'I could see that he was happy to show his emotion—those days of holding it in were well and truly gone. It was truly moving to see him honoured by the sport he had devoted so much to, and it gave him such a boost.'

The final between New Zealand and Australia was held in Melbourne, and Marty just had to go and watch. He particularly wanted to see Guppy and Ross Taylor—the two sons he never had—in action. They both meant a lot to him, especially Ross, with whom he shared a unique bond.

I didn't go to Melbourne for the final (which Australia won), and I wondered what condition Marty would be in when he got back to New Zealand. It was bound to have been emotionally draining for him.

When he got home we had one of our beautiful, deep talks. We'd always been able to talk openly to one another, but I could feel that connection more than ever: we were able to speak from the heart with no barriers at all. That's the thing about finding your soulmate—you know you can trust the other person to let you share whatever you need to. There's no judgement, just pure understanding.

That connection we had was so precious, and those heartfelt chats are one of the things I miss most now.

I asked Marty what he was feeling, now that the huge high he'd been on throughout the World Cup was over.

'What's next?' I asked.

'I've said my final goodbye to cricket,' he said. 'Now I'm thinking that I might try writing another book. But I also want to see Emma grow into a well-balanced, stunning young lady. And I want to be the best companion I can possibly be to you, Raine.'

He'd closed one door, and now it was time to open another one and enter the next stage in his life.

The day before we went to Sydney for the Cricket World Cup, I'd had my own health scare. I'd gone for my yearly mammogram, and I was asked to wait afterwards while my images were reviewed. The radiologist wasn't there, but there was a breast surgeon speaking in a very loud voice.

'I'll discuss Lorraine's scans with her,' she said.

I'd never met this surgeon before, and her manner was not reassuring. She took me into a small, dark room where an image of my right breast was displayed on a computer screen. In a very matter-of-fact tone, she told me that I had a lot of calcification in the breast and would need a biopsy.

She mentioned the word cancerous—some calcifications can be early signs of cancer—and I couldn't help asking the obvious question. What, in her expert opinion, was the chance I could have the disease?

She casually replied, 'Hmmm, seventy-five percent chance.'

I instantly felt sick. Seventy-five percent was very high. This was the last thing I needed.

Marty and I were bound for Sydney the next day, so I would have to wait until we got back in a couple of weeks to have the biopsy. I didn't sleep at all that night; swirling around in my head were the words 'seventy-five percent chance'.

Before we left for the airport, I rang my breast specialist, Dr Caroline Gray, and voiced my worries. As soon as she heard my story, she apologised for the comments the surgeon had made and told me to ignore that percentage.

'Most of the time, these biopsies come back as benign,' she said.

That made me feel a little better, but I still boarded the plane with the fear that I could have cancer hanging over me.

In the two weeks we were away, I decided it was my turn to walk the talk. Every day I said prayers of gratitude for everything I had in my life, and I repeated a positive affirmation: 'My breasts are healthy; my results will be benign.' Whenever I felt a spike of fear, I pushed it away with that affirmation.

> 'I didn't sleep at all that night; swirling around in my head were the words "seventy-five percent chance".'

I went for the biopsy on 1 April. Coincidentally, it was also the day I started promoting the Pink Ribbon Breakfast—a fundraiser for the Breast Cancer Foundation—on the media page of my website. I was feeling a little scared and couldn't wait for it to be over. While the staff prepared the room where I would be having the biopsy, I sat in a small waiting area, wearing the robe you get changed into for the procedure. It felt like the longest ten minutes of my life, and gave my anxiety plenty of time to build up.

Finally I was shown into the room. I had to lie on a table on my left side while my right breast was put into a mammogram machine and flattened like a fried egg. That was okay, but my outstretched left arm was very uncomfortable due to the reduced blood flow.

A number of images were taken, and then the specialist entered the room to do the biopsy. I couldn't see his face; I could only hear his voice. The radiographer said I could squeeze her hand while the specialist injected local anaesthetic into my breast. The next part was the most invasive bit of the whole procedure as the biopsy needle went in. Although it didn't hurt, I could feel the prodding. Three samples were removed, more images were taken, and finally a tiny metal clip was inserted for future reference in case they needed to go back to the biopsy site.

As I was released from the machine, the emotion overcame me and I burst into tears. The staff were kind and gentle, telling me it was okay to cry. I had been trying so hard to be brave since that first mammogram weeks earlier, when I was told there was a seventy-five percent chance of cancer. I had done my best not to worry, but when you store emotion like that, it has to come out some time.

For me, what made the whole procedure particularly bloody awful was that it was my breast being tugged and pulled. I've had more painful dentist's appointments, but this felt more invasive.

I asked to get the results as quickly as possible, and was told that they would be given to Caroline Gray the following day. Two hours before my appointment with her, the fear came knocking and I grew extremely anxious. I called Patricia, who talked me through it until I was peaceful again.

'You're not alone, Lorraine—God, your dad and Jean are walking with you,' she told me. Thanks to her, I felt calm as I left for the appointment.

The news Caroline had for me was great: the calcifications were benign and I did not have cancer. Again, I burst into tears, this time of relief. I was filled with gratitude, knowing that God continued to walk with me, ensuring that I never had to feel alone.

With God's help, I could get back to being there for my beautiful man.

Chapter Twenty

Marty's decision not to have more chemotherapy and to stay at home instead meant that it was time for him to visit Mercy Hospice.

When our doctor Anna Twhigg first suggested this, he responded with surprise.

'Oh, it's a long way from that, isn't it?'

At that stage he was still feeling quite strong, and he thought that you only went to hospice when you were in your last days.

Anna explained that hospices are not just places where people go to die; they offer a whole range of options for people facing life-limiting illnesses. These include at-home nursing care and twenty-four-hour phone access to advice, as well as counselling and family support. Patients can stay at hospice for pain management and to give caregivers some respite, as well as getting care in their final days. These services are free to the public, provided thanks to donations. It really is an incredible organisation.

So Marty agreed to visit Mercy Hospice. As soon as we stepped out of the elevator, we could sense a special energy about the place. The staff were wearing their own clothes, not uniforms, which made it feel more relaxed. There was an instant feeling of warmth, compassion and respect from everyone we met. I knew Marty was going to be well cared for.

We took up the hospice's offer of having the community nursing team visit Marty at home. He had three nurses, and Katie McGregor was the first. I will never forget opening the door to Katie, who has incredible penetrating blue eyes. She was young and upbeat, but also gently spoken when needed.

It was so important for Marty to have people around him with the right energy, and I knew Katie was going to be wonderful.

Susie Watkin was gorgeous too, with lovely sparkling eyes and a 'cool' bohemian feel. The last of the golden trio was the ever-stylish Anne Brown, who had a motherly warmth about her.

These three were the perfect people to have in our home, caring for Marty in the most intimate ways. They also trained me to administer his pain relief and nurse him when we were alone together.

Our hospice team would visit as often as we wanted, and I know that I couldn't have cared for Marty at home without their support. I became very close to these three earth angels, who not only cared for my husband but for me, too. There were times when it was a huge relief to open the door and see their angelic faces.

Having twenty-four-hour phone access to Mercy Hospice was also a lifeline—quite literally—because there were times when things happened that scared me. It was such a comfort knowing that help was at the other end of the phone, any time of the day or night.

One of the things I found scary was a drug called oxycodone, which Marty was put on for pain relief around June 2015. It was evil—it had a terrible effect on Marty's demeanour, making him very dark. Even his eyes went dark in colour. He just wasn't himself and it was a very challenging time for me, as it made me feel disconnected from him.

Thank God I had Marty's friend Dave and my lovely Patricia close by. Marty only felt comfortable with a small number of people, and those two were among them. They would come to the house when needed and support me, staying with Marty while I went for a walk to get some much-needed fresh air and exercise. By this time I had stopped my weekly yoga class; I couldn't concentrate when my mind was elsewhere, worrying about Marty.

The high level of oxycodone Marty was on was a concern, and he went to stay at Mercy Hospice so they could sort out his medication. While he was there he got an upsetting phone call, which left him so agitated that the staff gave him sedation to try to calm him down.

Marty said he wanted to go home, but the team looking after him were reluctant to let him leave until they had sorted out the drugs. I was having a meeting with one of the doctors when another staff member came in to tell us they couldn't find Marty.

Eventually he was located outside in the garden, even though it was very cold. One of the staff suggested he come back inside.

'I can't even go outside for some fresh air without feeling I am being checked on,' he said as he walked past me into the building. 'We are leaving as soon as I have my bag packed. Okay, you got that?'

That wasn't Marty talking, it was the oxycodone, but in that moment he meant it.

I needed help dealing with Marty when he was like that. In a panic, I rang Dave, hoping he could support me to keep Marty at the hospice until we could get his medication sorted out.

'Marty wants to go and I need you to come now; can you?' I asked.

'Of course,' he said. 'I'm on my way.'

Unfortunately, Dave misinterpreted my words. When I said Marty wanted to leave, he thought I meant that he was ready to pass from this world to the next! He grabbed his guitar so he could play to Marty in his final hours and rushed to the hospice, coming upon Marty alone in his room.

'Thank God you're here, we're leaving now,' said Marty.

Poor Dave was very confused. He had expected to find Marty taking his last breaths; instead he found himself being roped into busting Marty out of the hospice.

The two of them were heading to the lifts when I arrived with the medical team. It was a tricky situation; in the end the doctor said it was okay for Marty to leave, but first they needed to arrange the medication he'd require at home.

'She can bring it,' Marty said, pointing at me. 'See you.'

The lift doors opened and Marty walked in.

Dave looked at me for guidance, and I nodded for him to go

with Marty. As the doors were closing Dave mouthed 'sorry' to me.

The doctor suggested we go to a private room. As soon as he shut the door behind us, I burst into tears.

'Please tell me this has happened before with other patients?' I asked.

I was reassured that yes, it had happened before. They see it all at hospice.

Apparently Marty was determined to beat the peak-hour traffic home—it was almost five in the evening—and he had Dave driving his small Honda Civic at high speed around the waterfront. I got stuck in traffic, so it was 6.30 p.m. by the time I reached our house. I opened the front door to the sound of Michael Bublé blaring out of the speakers, and walked into the lounge to see Marty with a glass of wine in his hand, singing and swaying along to the music.

'Hi, darling,' he said, like nothing had happened. I could have killed him.

Dave was looking very nervous, as if he thought there could be an actual death at this stage.

I was about to lose it, but then I thought, *What will that achieve? Nothing.*

I poured myself a glass of wine.

'Let's draw a line under today and start again. What are we going to have for dinner?' I said.

The story of what happened that day came to be known as The Great Hospice Escape. It has been told many times, and it still makes me smile now.

Marty knew he wasn't himself on the oxycodone, and he wanted to have a scan to see what was happening with the lymphoma. It turned out that the tumour causing his pain had actually reduced in size, but there was a new growth in his stomach.

Marty being Marty, he decided to stop taking the oxycodone anyway and go cold turkey. So we retreated to Omaha, the town where we'd got married, this time staying at the home of a friend of Marty's sister Deb. She and her partner Grant hunkered down with us while Marty battled the withdrawals from the drug. It was awful to watch: he couldn't stop crying and had no energy, and this went on for days.

His recovery was slow, but eventually he started to feel more like himself. I could see the darkness had gone from his face, and his beautiful eyes were sparkling again. We had our Marty back.

For pain relief, he switched to morphine. It was a much better fit for his pain than oxycodone, which is similar to morphine but a synthetic version.

Marty was happier off the oxycodone but, bit by bit, parts of his life were being taken away. His energy was very low and he struggled to do even gentle activities. Going for walks together had always given us so much joy, but it got to the stage where this wasn't really possible. I would drive him to the beach, but he'd only get as far as the water's edge before saying, 'Okay, let's go home.'

He loved books but couldn't concentrate on reading, and whenever we tried watching movies together he would be asleep within fifteen minutes. Fortunately, he could still enjoy listening to music and he retained his appetite.

Witnessing what he was going through was often excruciatingly painful: the way he would sit with his head hung low; his gentle moans due to his aching body; his shuffling as he moved. His beautiful voice was gone and replaced with a whisper. I seldom saw his smile or glimpses of that cheeky nature I loved so much. My Marty was slipping away.

For me, the grim reality of what was happening was presenting itself more and more. I was trying to process the fact that our life together would never be the way it once was, and that one day soon he would be gone forever. I thought about what life was going to be like when he was gone, and wondered if I could survive my grief.

My dear friend Frances in Wellington continued to send me

beautiful bouquets every now and then, and they would seem to arrive at just the right time. The flowers were gorgeous and always in colours she knew I loved. I'd open the door when they were delivered and they'd take my breath away. Looking at them in the days that followed was a boost to my spirits. I felt so lucky to have such a kind and thoughtful friend, who seemed to know just when I needed a lift.

One of the other tricky things I had to cope with at this time was dealing with people who wanted to see Marty. A lot of people were keen to come and visit, including some old friends who hadn't been in touch for many years. But it wasn't always possible for Marty to see them—he had almost zero energy, and communicating with others could take a huge toll.

There was another factor, too: the spiritual work he had done over recent years had shown him what type of energy he wanted to be surrounded with. He could pick up on someone's vibe instantly, and he knew that some people would suck what little energy he had, while others would fill him with energy thanks to their presence. So there were some people he wanted there, and others he didn't. He became very protective of his space, especially as his energy levels were unpredictable from one day to the next. He would make the decision on any given day as to whether he would see people or not.

Sadly, some people who were told no took it very personally and couldn't understand why he wouldn't see them. In one or two cases, I got the blame.

Marty knew who his true friends were, and who he wanted around him in those last months. But sometimes it was me who had to deliver the message.

Dave was on constant standby and would come over whenever we needed him, sitting with Marty while I went to get groceries or run errands. One day while I was out I got a text from Marty that stopped me in my tracks.

'My incredible friend and soulmate, I am heartbroken and torn. I don't want to do this life with cancer any longer, and I don't want to give up in your eyes. I'm broken in two. Xx'

My reply was instant. 'My beautiful man, I don't want you to do this life with cancer either. It's heartbreaking for me as well. As I've said before, you are the one who has to walk your own path and you have to make your own decisions on how you do that. No one else can walk your path. So therefore whatever you decide, you have my full, loving support.

'In my eyes, you have been so brave and if you feel you want to stop fighting this battle, that is absolutely okay. I am here all the way with you, to love you and support your wishes. Eternally, forever yours, Raine.'

When I got home we held one another and cried for most of the day. We both knew he was going to let the cancer take him; there was no more fighting this. It hurt so much, and there was nothing I could do. I wished I could perform magic and make everything right again.

That evening, the reality of what was happening hit me like a hurricane. The emotion engulfed me to the point that I was physically sick. I had to take half an anxiety pill to calm myself down.

It truly sank in that a time was coming when I would no longer be able to see Marty, to feel him, hear him, smell him, touch him.

I knew that one day it would be just me in the house. He would no longer be there to smile at me, squeeze me, make me laugh. There would be nothing. I was going to be totally alone.

The last time I'd faced the prospect of being on my own, after the break-up of my first marriage, I'd had two small children to look after and keep me busy. Now Hilton and Jasmine were both off leading their own lives, and it would just be me.

I cried so much that every part of me hurt. The pain was terrible—and then came the numbness. What lay ahead seemed so grim and I felt empty. I wished my Jean was alive so that I could phone her and she could calm me down. But of course she was gone.

Marty did not see any of this; I hid the true extent of my grief from him. Although I actually began grieving before he died, I never let him see it. After my breakdown that night, I got up the next day and carried on with a smile on my face.

One day when Marty and I were talking, I told him that I wanted to come with him.

'I don't want to stay here without you. I've done everything: I've raised my beautiful children, I've had a successful business, I've had this beautiful love with you. I'm ready to go.'

My wise man knew what to say to me.

'Raine, you can't go. Your children still need you; your work as a mother is not finished.'

He was right, of course. There was still so much more for me to do. I couldn't leave Hilton and Jasmine and Emma.

But I do know that when the time does come for me to go, I won't be scared. I don't fear death. I believe in eternal life: that your physical body dies but your soul moves on to the next part of the journey in the spirit world. It is a beautiful place. I will be at peace when my time comes to go there, because Marty will be waiting for me, and that will be amazing.

Chapter Twenty-one

In November 2015 we decided to do some small trips within New Zealand, or at least to try. The first was to Hahei in the Coromandel; Marty hadn't been there before and I wanted him to see this stunningly beautiful area.

I booked an Airbnb right on the beach. Marty wasn't feeling great when we first arrived, so after a short walk he took some medication and went to bed; I spent the afternoon by the water. Ever since my childhood holidays at the Mount the beach has always been my happy place, and I felt relaxed and free as I strolled along the sand beside the sparkling blue sea.

That evening Marty was able to go to dinner at a local restaurant and, much to my delight, he consumed a huge meal.

On our last night there we sat outside on the grass overlooking the beach with an antipasto platter and some wine, watching the sky turn pink. We laughed like two teenagers in love and went to bed listening to the sound of the waves.

The weather was glorious the next morning and we managed a short walk up a hill. We held one another and admired the spectacular view in the stillness of the day.

After breakfast we decided that I should go for a walk to the famous Cathedral Cove. It would have been too much for Marty as the return trip takes about an hour and a half from Hahei, so I left him lying on a recliner at the Airbnb.

'Not bad, this retired life at fifty-three,' he joked.

Going on the walk was a mistake. The last time I'd done it was about fourteen years earlier with my sister Sue, and we'd been the only ones on the beach when we got to Cathedral Cove. This time I couldn't believe how many other people were there; it just didn't feel the same.

But the thing that really got to me was reflecting on how much Marty would have loved this walk. It occupied my mind the whole way there and back, and I felt so sad doing it alone. As I headed back towards the house, I got a really strong sense of what it would be like to be on my own permanently. I knew Marty was waiting for me back at the house now, but one day he wouldn't be.

I rushed back along the beach to the Airbnb, and felt so blessed to find him still there, and still alive.

5 November 2015 marked the tenth anniversary of Marty and I meeting one another again, and the beginning of our special love story. As we reminisced about those ten years, Marty made an observation.

'We've come from not being able to keep our hands off each other, to not being able to keep our eyes off each other.'

It was so true: there was so much we could say to one another with just a look.

We managed one more short trip away; this time to Waihi where Marty's close friend Foxy and his wife Adele had a bach by the water. As always, a long weekend at the beach helped to re-energise us both.

We did have another trip planned: to Wainui beach in Gisborne. But we never made it.

As Christmas approached, it was clear this was going to be Marty's last one. We all knew it, although nothing was said.

Christmas lunch was to be at the home of my sister Jenny and brother-in-law Pope. As Jasmine, Emma and I finished our preparations, Marty came down from the bedroom, all ready to go.

He was dressed up in the white suit he wore for our wedding, with a shirt in his favourite colour—orange—and a hat. That said it all.

In the New Year, Marty showed signs of being more and more ready to leave. His body retained a lot of fluid and he became very swollen. I was taught how to do lymphatic massage to help get rid of some of the fluid. It had to be done every day, so I would light more candles—we had scented candles burning 24/7—and gently massage him.

As I stroked his swollen body, I would be overwhelmed with love for this man. His illness was hideous, but there was much that it gave me, too. It made me a more compassionate human being, and it allowed me to go to a place in my soul that I hadn't touched before. Our relationship reached a place of total purity, of deep soul love. We couldn't have been any closer. We were always in the present moment together.

If ever we felt ourselves getting upset with one another, we would instantly move to make it better, knowing every second was vital. We had to be 'in-spirit'—as we used to say at the beginning of our relationship—for every moment. Time was running out.

Emma would come over each day and, depending on Marty's energy levels, spend a few hours with him talking or playing backgammon. No matter how awful he was feeling, his eyes would light up when she entered the room. He absolutely adored his beautiful girl, and the feeling was mutual: she loved her papa so very, very much.

A year earlier Marty had begun working on a journal for Emma, full of his thoughts about life and love. He wrote down his advice, trying to cover everything he thought she would need for the rest of her life—what he would have said to her if he had still been there. She meant the world to him.

Emma was so brave, and never showed the grief she must have been feeling. Instead she always arrived with a beautiful smile and a loving heart. She is one of the most courageous young women I have ever known.

Marty and Emma playing one of their many games of backgammon.

Marty had asked Dave to oversee his funeral the previous year, and told him what he wanted. Initially he requested a black coffin with a silver fern on it, and my immediate thought was: *No, that's not right for you.* Maybe it was the colour consultant in me coming out, but black was not his colour; it had never represented him.

'So we're going to be looking at a coffin that is going to be a reflection of you, and it's going to be black?' I queried.

He thought about it, then changed his mind.

'What was I thinking? I don't want Emma sitting there looking at a huge black coffin. It's got to be orange. And it's got to have a love heart with the date we were married, and a monarch butterfly with the date Emma was born.'

I was glad. He wanted the theme of his funeral to be 'Basking in the sun' and orange was a much better colour.

Dave came over for a meeting about the funeral and I made notes as they talked, writing down the people Marty wished to carry his personally designed coffin and all the other details. As I was compiling a list of the family and friends he wanted at his private cremation, I looked at the names and realised with a shock that Marty's was missing. It sounds crazy, but it hit me hard in that moment that he would not be there. It was like being struck by a thunderbolt.

We made it to our seventh wedding anniversary on 14 February 2016. Marty gave me a journal with some beautiful love notes, and we put on our favourite movie, *The Bridges of Madison County*. We cuddled up together, holding hands and knowing in our hearts how blessed we had been to find one another.

After a short while Marty was asleep and I continued to watch the movie alone, nursing my glass of champagne. I could only have one; as his caregiver my alcohol intake was limited because I had to administer his drugs.

In his last months Marty was sleeping in the living room on a hospital bed organised by our wonderful hospice nurse Anne; I would lie on a mattress next to him. I needed to be close so that I could bring him pain relief as soon as he needed it. We didn't get a lot of sleep, and would be up all hours of the night having cups of tea and long chats. Even now, I still haven't returned to sleeping a full night.

On the evening of 1 March, we had a night from hell. His pain was unbearable and I had to give him continuous drugs to help him through it. The next morning, he awoke with a new pain in his side that he'd never felt before. I couldn't get on top of it with the medication, and when I rang Mercy Hospice they told me to bring him in for evaluation.

'We didn't get a lot of sleep, and would be up all hours of the night having cups of tea and long chats.'

'We've got to go to hospice so they can sort out your pain relief; we'll just be there for the night,' I said to Marty.

He didn't like having to go in, but this time there was no resistance.

'Okay,' he replied simply.

Marty wasn't keen to go in an ambulance, so I called Dave and asked if he could help me get him into the car. When Dave arrived, Marty asked us to wait a little.

'Just give me an hour and we'll go,' he said.

While I was out of the room Marty had a question for Dave. 'You will come and visit Raine after I'm gone?'

He knew the end was approaching.

I gave Marty a shot of morphine and we drove to the hospice, with Dave following in the car behind. I always have music playing in the car and Marty was singing and grooving away; he seemed so happy. We laughed as we drove and he directed me on which way he wanted to go.

At the hospice, Dave helped Marty out of the car and towards the front door. Marty stopped and leant on his friend.

'Just slowly, Morrie, I'm struggling a bit here,' he said, using his affectionate nickname for Dave (from the surname Morris).

Marty was smiling and calm as he stepped out of the lift and said hi to everyone, which is not something he usually did. Looking back now, I can see that he knew this was it.

As we settled him into his room, Marty said we needed our rest because we had a big week coming up. At the time I thought he was referring to our possible trip to Wainui beach. But he was talking about his funeral.

Marty slept for most of the day and the intense pain seemed to settle. *Oh, it's a false alarm*, I thought. *This has just been another episode of pain and thankfully it has passed.*

We watched *Shortland Street* together, and I popped out to buy him some fruit juice, nuts and liquorice in case he needed anything in the night.

By 9 p.m. Marty was sleeping, so I decided to go home and try for some rest myself. I kissed him goodbye and texted him a message.

'I've gone home to get some sleep, call me when you wake up.' He never saw that message.

The staff assured me that if there was any change they would let me know.

On the drive home, I sat at the traffic lights observing people crossing in front of me, laughing with happiness while I was filled with grief. In that moment I saw how joy and sorrow can co-exist in life. I understood that you never know what others around you may be going through.

I went to bed as soon as I got home, but at about 10.30 p.m. I awoke with a jolt, sensing that something was wrong. I rang the hospice to check on Marty; his nurse said the pain had returned and he had been up and about.

'Should I come in?' I asked.

I was told they had his pain under control, and I should get some sleep.

'Okay, but call me if anything happens.'

When my phone rang at 2.45 a.m. and I saw that it was Mercy Hospice, I knew.

'You need to come now, Lorraine, there's been a big change,' his nurse said.

I called Marty's sister Deb, who lived in Matakana, about an hour north of Auckland. She picked up after one ring. We had never discussed this moment but I knew she would want to be there, and I needed her. She had been on this journey with both of us.

I changed into the first items of clothing I could lay my hands on and drove to the hospice, knowing that the very thing I feared was now happening and there was nothing I could do about it.

> 'I sat at the traffic lights observing people crossing in front of me, laughing with happiness while I was filled with grief. In that moment I saw how joy and sorrow can co-exist in life.'

At 3.15 a.m. I arrived to find Marty in a semi-coma and breathing rapidly.

'Oh, my darling, what's happened?' I said. I held his hand and told him to blink his eyes or squeeze my hand if he could hear me.

He blinked his eyes.

I sat with him and talked to him until Deb arrived and we fell into one another's arms. She was very close to her brother, who loved her dearly.

The doctor who was treating Marty told us that he could go at any time. It could be one hour or two; one day or two. We made the phone calls we needed to make: his mum Audrey, our close family, Dave and Patricia. Soon he was surrounded by his loved ones. Dave arrived wearing a T-shirt of Marty's that Marty had given him. It said, 'Keep the faith and believe in truth'. Such perfect words.

Everyone was able to have their own personal moment with Marty, which was wonderful.

Dave and Patricia at Marty's bedside during his final hours. Dave was playing his guitar.

Marty was moaning but the medical team reassured us that he wasn't in pain; it was a sign that his body was shutting down. Patricia, who is gifted spiritually, turned to me.

'He's on his way and trying to say his goodbyes to us. I don't think he wants to go, Lorraine.'

So I told him, 'It's okay to go now, honey; it's time.'

The room was cleared of everyone apart from me so that the nurses could give him a wash. As we were turning him over, he let out a loud moan.

'Lorraine, he is going,' a nurse said to me.

I asked her to call in his loved ones from the next room, and as they came in I held Marty's head in my hands.

'You are so loved, my beautiful man,' I told him. 'This is not over yet. This is so not over.'

I meant that our love was not over; it had just been cut short and we would reunite again one day.

'Go into the light, go to your dad and Jean,' I told him.

Marty then took his last breath, and as he did his face looked angelic, all soft and fuzzy. I witnessed his spirit leaving his body.

'Did you see that?' I asked the others.

They didn't, but I did, and it was unbelievably peaceful and beautiful.

Marty died at 11.40 a.m. on 3 March 2016. He was fifty-three. We were able to stay with him in the room at Mercy Hospice until 4 p.m. We lit a candle and shared stories about him while sharing a bottle of red wine that my brother-in-law Pope had gone to get. Marty loved a good red.

In the time we had together before he passed, I said my own private goodbye to the most brave, beautiful, kind-hearted man I have ever known. He had done so much courageous work on himself, and finally found his peace. He left this earth calmly, knowing that he was so loved.

Chapter Twenty-two

Throughout Marty's cancer journey, there were two very special people who were with us both from beginning to end. Dave Morris and Patricia Adams walked every step of that journey and never faltered. They made it clear to me and Marty that they would do anything we needed at any stage, and they never let us down.

Marty loved them both very much and enjoyed their company; they lifted his energy whenever they were around. From day one they had an 'all-access' pass to Marty and he was always happy to see them.

Dave and Patricia were there for me too when I needed help and support. They witnessed everything, including Marty's passing. Even in the really hard times, their friendship never wavered, nor did their ability to 'hold the space' for me and Marty: to sit with us and just be still, allowing us to do whatever we needed to do—whether that was crying, yelling, or saying nothing at all. Dave and Patricia are true angels.

The four of us shared a faith in God, and in a love that knows no limits. I will be forever grateful to them both; they saved us many times when things got tough. Through the power of faith in love and eternity, we made it. We delivered Marty safely to his next journey.

On the evening of the day Marty died, I sat down at home with close family to watch the TV news. I wanted to see how they shared the information of his passing. When Jonah Lomu had died back in November, Marty and I watched the news together and exchanged a look; we were both thinking that one day there would be a news item about Marty's passing.

I watched the main two channels and both went into detail about his cricketing achievements, but there was no mention of the fact that Marty was a father. It made me angry. He never wanted to be defined only by his cricketing career.

When Marty had asked me to speak at his funeral, I was worried that I wouldn't be able to do it because I would be too grief-stricken. But after watching those news items, I knew I had to get up and talk about the real Marty. There would be TV cameras there; I had so much to share about Marty the husband, the father, the son, the friend, the peaceful man he was at the end of his life. I knew it was going to be hard, but I had to do it.

Marty had planned his funeral in such detail that it seemed like there would be little to do, but in fact it amazed me how much we had to deal with in the week leading up to the event. Marty had decided to have a public service that was broadcast live, as there was worldwide media interest. Lou Henderson, our wonderful manager, did an incredible job of overseeing it all. My close friends circled around me as the day approached, loving and protecting me.

I had been feeling pretty grounded, but the day before the funeral I woke up with the sense that I was flying around the room with emotion. I couldn't centre myself, and there was no way I wanted to be in that state the next day.

I called Peter Caughey, our acupuncturist and good friend, who was back in New Zealand from his home in Bali. Marty and I considered Peter one of our trusted spiritual mentors, and he kindly agreed to come and see me that day. We sat in the sun, talking about the funeral. Peter said it should be a joyous occasion because it was a celebration of love.

'Lorraine, this is your opportunity to share Marty with everyone—the true Marty—and the very special love you had.

Many people never get to experience a love like that at such a deep, soul level. It's a wonderful thing to be able to let others see that.'

He told me that Marty had given me a parting gift, which was to take me to another level of consciousness. I understood what he meant by this: I had changed throughout this journey and I saw everything now with new eyes. There was no going back.

When Peter left an hour later, I was calm and ready for the next day. I woke on the morning of the funeral still feeling serene. As I got up to speak in front of the hundreds of people who attended the service at the Holy Trinity Cathedral, I knew I was being carried by angels.

I talked about how Marty and I met, and how, from day one, he allowed me to truly just be me. I described him as passionate, romantic, fun and as cheeky as hell, and said that I knew we were the perfect match when I first saw his wardrobe and noticed he owned even more clothes and shoes than me.

I shared how he was a wonderful papa to Emma. 'Being a father was his greatest achievement and it brought him the most pleasure out of anything he ever did in his life. He also embraced my two children, Hilton and Jasmine, as though they were his own, in his own gentle way.'

It was important to talk about how his illness had changed him. 'The hideous cancer that took him from us also saved him,' I said. 'The cancer gave him the opportunity to stop and sit still and find out who he really was.

'In the past, before the cancer, sometimes Marty could be intense, restless and, as the media reported recently, complex. He was not afraid to publicly voice his thoughts and this was sometimes misunderstood.

'I will say to those people who didn't "get" Marty: his intention always came from a place of integrity and absolute truth. He was the most honest man I have ever met.'

I explained how he'd done the courageous work of facing himself, and how he had finally seen what we all knew about him—that he was a gentle, kind and loving soul.

Then I spoke to Marty.

'I will be forever grateful to you, my darling, for what you shared with me, for helping me to grow as a person, for showing me what living in the moment means, and what being loved and cherished truly feels like.

'You loved me in a way that I have never been loved. It will never be forgotten.'

I made it through my speech without a hitch. In fact, the whole service went according to plan (just about) and was everything Marty had wished for. He wanted it to be about basking in the sun—those words were written on the service sheet—and it was a beautiful sunny day.

Marty's brother Jeff and his great cricketing friend Ian Smith both spoke beautifully, and Dave sang a moving song he had written himself. There were touching video tributes from the two sons he never had, Ross Taylor and Martin Guptill, who were in India with the Black Caps for the World Twenty20.

After the service we followed the orange coffin out into the courtyard of the cathedral, the sun shining down on us, and boys from Marty's school (Auckland Grammar) performed a powerful and emotional haka. Then there was a stillness as his coffin was placed in the hearse.

As the car moved away, that's when it hit me big-time that he was gone. Hilton and Jasmine held me in their arms—Hilton being strong for his mother, and Jasmine in tears for a man she had a very special bond with.

Parts of the day are a blur, but I do remember standing in the area where tea and sandwiches were being served as a line formed of people wanting to speak to me. It amazed me how long some of those people waited, just to be able to talk with me for a short moment about our beautiful Marty.

The private cremation was held afterwards and, for me, it was the highlight of the day. Family and close friends shared their precious memories of Marty, including his mother Audrey who read the last message Marty had sent to her phone.

Dave read out two pieces Marty had written to Emma and me.

'Raine, you walked back into my life in November 2005 like

a karmic angel,' he wrote to me. 'You saw in me what nobody else could see. When we married on Valentine's Day in 2009 I entered a real euphoria, where love enveloped me through the vow ceremony and beyond.

'My vow "I will always love you well" was my authentic truth. Gratefully, we were side by side, facing in the same direction. I love you eternally, Raine.'

To Emma he wrote, 'At the end, I found meaning in my life. It came through Raine and you. My gift back to you is to know that whenever you need a meaning on anything, always choose love, and the meaning will be there. Love always finds a way.'

Afterwards, the small group of family and friends came back to our house to continue celebrating Marty's life until the wee hours of the following day, with great food, wine, happy stories and dancing. We knew that was exactly what Marty would have wanted us to do.

One of the stories told that night to much hilarity related to events that took place after Marty died. On the Wednesday before Friday's funeral, at a dinner to discuss last-minute details, I suggested it might be wise for the pallbearers to practise lifting the coffin. Judging by previous funerals I'd been to, it looked like quite a tricky thing to do.

Grant Fox and Marty's cousin Russell weren't going to be in Auckland until the morning of the funeral, but the remaining four pallbearers—Marty's brother Jeff, stepson Hilton and friends Dave Morris and Steve Wilkins—could go to the funeral parlour the next day to have a run-through.

Steve had joked privately, 'Seriously, how difficult is it to pick up a coffin?' (Jeff nearly choked on his wine when he heard this) but given that the funeral was going to be broadcast live on two TV channels, they decided it was probably a good idea.

So they turned up to the funeral parlour the next day, expecting a rather sombre half hour. Steve related how they were instructed by the funeral directors (two of whom stood in for Foxy and Russell) to approach the coffin with their backs to the congregation, pick the coffin up using their closest arm, then pivot 180 degrees until they were facing the crowd with the coffin up on their shoulders.

This took a number of goes to get right—they butchered the first couple of attempts. After several more lifts Hilton asked why the coffin was so heavy, to which Jeff and Steve replied in unison, 'Because Marty's in there, you muppet!'

It took them a few moments to regain their composure after that. Then on the very next lift, Jeff passed wind as they lifted Marty up!

They broke out in hysterics, and basically didn't stop for the next thirty minutes. The sombre half hour had turned into a session of much-needed therapeutic laughter.

The group decided to practise walking with the coffin. While they were doing that, Jeff, Dave and Steve recalled a skit by comedian Dave Allen (one of Marty's favourites) in which pallbearers of different heights ended up tripping each other and dropping their cargo, the body falling out.

That led to a discussion about the possibility of something similar happening to them on live TV, and once again they were all in stitches.

Finally, they rehearsed lowering the coffin and holding it by the handles at waist level for a couple of minutes, which they would have to do when they came out of the church and the haka was performed. The sweaty palms broke out and, with hot weather forecast for the next day, they realised there could be a problem holding on to the coffin. Dave was particularly concerned. There was more banter about dropping Marty on live TV, and everyone ended up in fits of laughter again. Steve pointed out that weightlifters use chalk or talcum powder to help with grip, but no one appeared to take him seriously.

The whole session was very light-hearted, and I'm sure it helped the four of them feel a lot better about the responsibility of being pallbearers the following day.

Before the funeral, Steve had a chance to take a very emotional Foxy through the process of lifting the coffin, but unfortunately there was no time to brief Russell, who flew in from Australia that morning.

Marty and Foxy on a happier occasion: the day of my wedding to Marty. Photo by *The Australian Women's Weekly*.

As the service was winding down, the pallbearers started feeling a little anxious about their duty. Steve looked across at Dave, just in time to see him take a small bottle of talcum powder out of his wife Liz's bag and sprinkle it on his hands. He was clearly still worried about having sweaty palms and dropping the coffin.

The moment came, and they headed for their positions. Without the benefit of a rehearsal, Russell stood in the wrong position, so Dave kindly directed him into the right place with a gentle pat on the back.

Russell was wearing a new tailored Giorgio Armani suit, and I quickly spotted that he now had a lovely talcum powder handprint right in the middle of his jacket. My perfectionist tendencies kicked in—I was desperate to reach out and brush it off. But there was no way I could do that at this particular moment, so the photos of Russell from behind show the back of his beautiful suit adorned with talcum powder.

He took it with good grace, and had a laugh about it with Jeff, Foxy, Dave, Steve and Hilton over a glass of red after the service. It became known as the 'Hand on Armani' story and has since been told many times. Marty would have loved it.

The day after the funeral and our celebration at home, the family cleaning-up crew arrived to help me sort out the house. Someone mentioned that the flowers from the church were sitting outside by the garage and should be brought in out of the sun.

I went to get them, and couldn't believe my eyes when a monarch butterfly flew over and settled on the flowers. I called out to Emma and together we watched the butterfly in awe.

Marty had told us to look for monarch butterflies once he passed, and take them as a sign that he was always around us. He loved monarchs—which is why he had one on his coffin with Emma's birthdate—as well as anything orange.

We watched it together, knowing that my beautiful man and her beloved papa was with us still.

Chapter Twenty-three

During one of the intimate talks Marty and I had in his last year, I said to him, 'I don't know how I am going to keep going without you. How will I cope?'

'You will,' he replied. 'Just keep moving, Raine, remember that. Just keep moving.'

I thought of his words as the days and then weeks passed after his death. We had been living in a cocoon for the past year. Yes, Marty was dying—and dealing with the horrible things cancer does to a person physically—but in another way it was a beautiful period of our life together. We were living for each day, truly valuing our precious moments with one another and our loved ones. Life was good even though it was awful, and I felt blessed to have had that time with Marty. We had done the things we wanted to do, only venturing out to places where we felt relaxed and safe, and we had spent time with people who were important to us. We had talked and talked and talked.

In that year, I knew what my role was: to love my soulmate and help him deal with his illness until he passed. I had a purpose.

Now Marty was gone and I was lost. Who was I now? What did I want to do with my life? And how was I going to get through it without Marty beside me?

Shortly before he died, Marty had told me that after he was gone it would be my turn to put myself first and discover who I was.

'You can reinvent yourself,' he said. 'You can be a little selfish for a change; bask in the sun a little. Watch over your children and Emma, and find joy in that. This will be your time.'

Okay, I decided. That's what I would do. I would take time out to work out who I was and what I wanted to do.

Just keep moving, Raine.

The trouble with moving on after losing someone you love is that grief comes along and tries to stop you in your tracks. It leaves you with a deep longing that invades every cell of your body; a longing for something you can't have. I missed Marty so much I felt sick.

Yes, I had started mourning before he even died, but this grief was ten times worse. I wished he could come back for just an hour so I could hold him in my arms, touch him, smell him, kiss him and tell him how much it hurt without him. I missed his twinkly eyes, his warm smile, and his brave spirit. He had desperately wanted to stay as long as possible for me and Emma, his beloved girls.

I missed talking to him the most. I missed our conversations about anything and everything, the laughter and the cheekiness. There was so much I wanted to tell him, and so much I wanted to ask, too. Was he in a lot of pain in those final hours? Could he hear my voice? Did he understand what I was saying? Could he see me now?

And of course I wanted to know where he was, and what it was like there.

I kept thinking about how much relief I would get from being able to talk to him and touch him, even just for an hour.

But who was I kidding? An hour would not be enough. I would never want to let him go again.

Nearly four weeks after Marty died I sent a text to members of my family and close friends, trying to sum up what I was feeling.

'I am filled with such a deep longing to see him again, to hold him, to smell him, to kiss him and hear his voice. These feelings arrive in between the actual moments of everyday existence. I can feel normal and then my grief hits me and I have no choice but to sit with that grief. I filter back into my reality again when the grief has passed, or when I don't want to sit with it any longer.

'I can only be very gentle with myself, expecting nothing more than honouring what I am feeling in any given moment. I am surrounded by loving family and dear friends so I don't feel alone, but no one can do anything to help me process my grief. Only I (and time) can do that.'

It was a case of taking each day at a time and, as hard as that was, I had no choice but to do it. There's a saying attributed to Bob Marley that particularly resonates with me. It's about inner strength, and how you only discover the depth of yours when you've got no other option.

It is impossible for other people to understand what you go through when you lose your soulmate, unless they have been there themselves. Even then, it's not the same: grief is a unique experience for everyone. Nobody should ever attempt to tell you how to navigate that path. You have to do it your own way.

I found it hard when people asked me lots of questions. What was I going to do now? Would I sell the house? When would I go back to work?

I needed to be able to make decisions in my own time. Being questioned often felt like an interrogation, and I had no answers.

Another problem is that people start telling you what they think you should do, and that can be even tougher to deal with. One of the reasons it was so good having Patricia around was that she never told me what to do. The only question she ever asked was, 'How are you today?' She allowed me to just 'be' with whatever emotions I was experiencing, and she never pressured me.

If there was one thing worse than people questioning me and telling me what to do, it was when I ran into someone who had known Marty and they didn't say a word about him. They obviously didn't know what to say to me, but to say nothing at all just felt plain weird and uncomfortable; I think it's better to acknowledge his passing. I wished they would just say something about my beautiful man.

I found it easier when someone would look me straight in the eye and say, 'Lorraine, I am so sorry for your loss.' That gave me two choices: I could say 'thank you' and move the conversation on, or I could express a bit more about how I was feeling. It put the ball in my court.

It was hard when people said, 'Oh, I'm so sorry, how are you coping?' That could be a tricky question to answer—partly because it would trigger my emotions, but also because of the truth about how much I was struggling. I couldn't be sure they really wanted to hear that.

One thing I found helpful in those first weeks after Marty passed was reading the thoughtful messages in the many condolence cards I received. Rather than just a generic note, personal words about Marty were lovely to read, and I really appreciated them. In some cases, those messages meant more to me than their authors will ever know.

I also appreciated it when I could see that people had gone to a bit of trouble choosing their sympathy card. The cards that were visually beautiful always lifted my mood and provided some comfort. Little things like that made a big difference.

Something else people say to the recently bereaved is 'Let me know if I can do anything.' I know those words are kindly meant, but often nothing comes of them. The grieving person may be incapable of reaching out, or they may be unsure if the offer is genuine.

If you really want to help, make an offer that's specific: 'Would you like to come to dinner next weekend?' or 'I'll come over on Saturday to help you with the garden, if that's okay with you.'

Your friend can always say no if they're not feeling up to it, but at least they haven't had to be the one to make the approach. And if they do say no because they're not quite ready, follow up later with another offer.

Keep extending the hand of friendship. That person may need it more than you realise.

I was so lucky that my family and friends wrapped me in their love. My sister Jen and her husband Pope offered to take me to Sydney for a holiday. Hilton was living there at the time so it gave me a chance to go and see him.

I went to Sydney again later to spend a weekend with my dear friend Louise Calabro, who had come from LA to visit family. It was lovely to catch up with Louie, but as soon as I got back to Auckland and walked into my house I felt very alone. The place seemed so empty, and it hurt to see Marty's clothes still hanging in our wardrobe. I cleared them out, keeping a few of my favourite pieces and the ones that still smelled of him.

> 'The place seemed so empty, and it hurt to see Marty's clothes still hanging in our wardrobe. I cleared them out, keeping a few of my favourite pieces and the ones that still smelled of him.'

My lovely Wellington crew—Frances, Kath and Deb—invited me down to the capital for a weekend. It was a relief to let them look after me and make me laugh. But back home in Auckland I was on my own again, and I ached with loneliness.

A bit further down the track, I hosted a lunch for the Crowe family. Spending time with them was wonderful, but sad at the same time. I had such a strong connection with Marty's family; they truly understood what he meant to me. They knew how tough it was for me without him because they were missing him too. He left a big hole in all our lives.

When my manager Lou presented me with some work opportunities, there was no way I could contemplate saying yes. Friends and acquaintances started asking when I was going to go back to work, and I would feel myself tensing up. Other people might be able to bury themselves in their jobs but that wasn't going to work for me. My role as an image consultant requires a huge amount of energy—it's all about helping others find their confidence and building them up—and at this stage I had no energy left to give. I was exhausted with grief; I needed time to find my way through it. Lou suggested that I take a year off to do some things for me. Thank goodness my savings allowed me to do that.

With my energy very low, I booked acupuncture sessions with Peter Caughey. As always, he shared his wisdom with me.

'The pain you're feeling is a pure expression of love,' he said at one session. 'The greater the love, the greater the grief.'

Peter understood exactly what it was like to have someone you love ripped from your life—his son Daniel had died at the age of just nineteen.

Another time, Peter warned me not to try to do too much; he said it could take a serious toll on me. He also told me to beware of people who wanted to connect just so they could feel better about Marty's death.

'If you feel drained when you're around certain people, it's because they are taking your energy,' he said. I knew which people he meant.

'Try to spend time with people who expect nothing and allow you to be yourself,' he advised. 'They will energise you.'

Peter's words made sense and his wisdom brought me comfort, but still the pain persisted. I pressed on, and got into a routine of doing a yoga sequence at the start of every day. But one morning on my yoga mat, a wave of grief came out of nowhere and drove me to my knees, sobbing.

Other people get cancer and survive—why did it have to take Marty? Why did he have to leave me?

I knew that by the end it had made him so sick that he couldn't go on; there was just no way. But sometimes it was hard to accept.

About five weeks after Marty died, I invited our three Mercy Hospice nurses over for afternoon tea. I wanted to say thank you to Katie, Susie and Anne for everything they did for Marty and for me. We all shed tears as they shared their stories about caring for him, and talked about how much they liked him.

It was nice to learn that they had loved coming to our home and watching me with Marty; they could tell we were soulmates. They told me that all they ever saw from me was love towards Marty, and that they had noticed how I never complained. I was glad to hear that; I would not have wanted Marty to hear me moaning about anything.

I had asked Katie to bring Marty's file from Mercy Hospice as I had some questions about his final hours. I wanted to know what had happened in the time between me going home and getting the phone call to say he was nearing the end.

They told me that Marty wasn't anxious in the hours after I left, and that he had been out of bed for a short while and spoken politely to staff. The deterioration in his breathing was a sign that the process of dying had started and his body was shutting down; his brain was trying to tell his lungs how to breathe.

Some people can last like that for days, but not Marty. For him, the end came quickly. The last groan he let out before he died was not pain, but an attempt to connect with me to say goodbye. The nurses reassured me that he was not in pain at this stage—there was no sign of hunched shoulders or a furrowed brow.

It was a comfort for me to know that what I had seen was all part of a natural process, and that he hadn't suffered.

These three women had become such an important part of our lives. They joined us on a very personal journey, sharing their knowledge and skills at a time when we were entering an unknown world. I put my trust in them instantly, and thanks to their teaching I was able to care for Marty at home. I will be forever grateful to these earth angels—and to the hospice service that brought them to us.

One of the things I struggled with was the fact that I had lost not only Marty, but 'us' as well. I missed being him and me, Marty and Raine. He made me feel adored and special, and now that was gone. Marty had promised in our wedding vows to love me well, and he had honoured that. All I could do was be thankful that I had experienced that kind of love; I know that many people aren't so lucky.

Marty filled my mind and my heart for practically 100 percent of my waking hours. In every situation I would find myself thinking, *What would Marty's reaction to this be? What would he say?*

Despite my decision not to rush back to work, I did agree to take on one new client who wanted her colours done and some help with her wardrobe. Two months after Marty passed, I spent a long day doing a shopping prep session for her. By the end of it I was bone-tired, and as I drove home I imagined walking into the house to find Marty waiting for me. He'd give me a kiss and a cuddle and we'd chat about my day over a glass of wine. He'd be able to re-energise me and make me laugh with his cheeky humour.

I could picture this whole scenario so clearly, but of course when I got home the house was empty. He was never going to be there again.

Whenever that reality hit me, it would feel as if I would be broken forever. I would wonder how I could carry on, and I'd have to remind myself of Marty's advice.

Keep moving, Raine, keep moving.

LIVE

Chapter Twenty-four

When my marriage to Murray broke up and I was struggling with grief and loneliness, my wise friend Jean had given me a tip.

'Lorraine, whatever you do, don't start drinking in the evenings on your own.'

I followed her advice then, and I needed to remember it again now that I had lost Marty. There were times when I desperately wanted some way of easing the hurt, but I knew that alcohol was not it. The first glass might relax me, a second might help to numb the pain, but a third would totally intensify it. Drinking only made things worse, and the next day it would leave me feeling slow and low in energy, which was the last thing I needed.

Jean had been right: no matter how tempting it might seem to dull my emotions with alcohol, it was a bad trap to fall into, and I stopped keeping wine in the fridge.

I had to think of other ways of combating the pain. Once again I turned to the coping mechanisms that had helped me through other tough times in my life, including the years when Marty was ill.

Going for a walk was one of the simplest options, and served the double purpose of exercising my body and exposing me to nature's calming influence. I was grateful to live close to a park and a beach, two places where I could soak in the beautiful surroundings.

I practised restorative yoga poses every day at home, as well as going to classes with the gifted Karla Brodie. I would walk out of her lessons feeling light and revived—there was never any

Jean sharing a moment with me on the day of my wedding. She always had wise words to pass on. Photo by *The Australian Women's Weekly*.

tightness afterwards, even if I had been sore at the start. I also took up spin classes again, and would leave each session in a much better frame of mind. It felt good to move.

I made myself go to tango milongas, even on those cold winter evenings when it was tempting to stay at home on the couch. Once I got there I always felt uplifted and energised, and it helped to take my mind off my grief and longing for Marty.

Music was my saviour on many an occasion. There are certain songs guaranteed to help me feel better: Tina Turner's 'Something Beautiful Remains', Stevie Wonder's 'Don't You Worry 'bout a Thing' and Sade's 'By Your Side' are among them. Whitney Houston's 'Step By Step' could have been written with me in mind. The familiar lyrics resonated with me, and the music connected me to Marty because he was a music lover, too.

A few months after Marty died, I went to see my trusted clairvoyant Angel Andrea. Marty came through, and she told me he was there to help me heal.

'When you feel that you cannot face the day, take a deep breath and fill up on his love and light. You will be able to take those steps you need to take, with Marty beside you.'

Andrea told me that Marty's love was all around me, and that he hugged me all the time. Those words we had used to describe our connection—being 'in-spirit' with one another—were even more meaningful now.

Then Andrea said that Marty wanted her to mention a song to me: Nat King Cole's 'Smile'. It was Marty's gift to me, she added.

I thought about the lyrics to the song, when Nat sings about smiling through your heartbreak. Those words were so appropriate. I was trying to smile, but it wasn't easy.

Not long afterwards, I went out for dinner with some people who asked a lot of questions about what I was going to do with my future. I got into my car at the end of the night feeling overwhelmed and vulnerable. For a minute or two I just sat behind the wheel, tears streaming down my face. Then I turned on the engine.

The song that came on was 'Smile' by Nat King Cole. In that moment, I knew that Marty was with me.

Like the yoga poses, having a soak in the bath became part of my daily routine. I lit candles and played music, and used the time to meditate. It helped to relax my body and mind, and made it easier to sleep.

I knew that in order to heal I had to look after myself, and that meant getting enough sleep as well as exercising and eating well. There were days when I would feel I was making progress, and then others when I was so fragile I thought I might shatter.

One day I was in Marty's office looking at the photos on his computer, which were playing in a continuous slideshow. I felt sick with loss as I watched the images of him appear. There he was, my beautiful man, so happy and healthy. And now he was gone.

I lay down on the rug in the sunshine and wrapped my head in a blanket, a nurturing move I had learned in yoga, and focused on drawing deep breaths up from my belly. I asked God to take away my sadness and fill me with love and white light. Gradually, as I listened to a guided meditation while the sun warmed my body, I began to feel calm, and the sick feeling in my stomach subsided.

It was encouraging to know that there were things I could do to help myself heal.

More than ever, I was thankful for my faith. I needed that strong belief I've always had in a divine energy force, and when I prayed I could feel a presence full of love. Whatever you call it—Buddha, Jesus, Allah or God—this higher power was there to help me through my darkest moments. The love I felt from this presence calmed me and filled me with peace, and I knew that I was never truly alone.

This divine love saved me; it got me through the heartache and made me hopeful that I would find joy again.

I went on several trips away in the months after Marty passed. As well as Wellington and Sydney, I spent time in Queenstown and Melbourne with friends and family. Having a change of scenery was a big help, and I knew that I was fortunate to have the resources to do this.

In September, Jasmine was heading to Los Angeles to attend

some dance classes, and I decided to go with her. Being able to watch her dance was bliss for me, and we had a wonderful week together. The grief that had been dogging me seemed to have eased until I was only dimly aware of it.

On the day before Jasmine was due to fly back to Australia (I was staying on in the States to visit friends) we went shopping in the city. As we walked down the busy street I was suddenly struck with the gut-wrenching realisation that Marty had died—as if it had only just happened.

'As we walked down the busy street I was suddenly struck with the gut-wrenching realisation that Marty had died—as if it had only just happened.'

I went back to our Airbnb for a nap, and when I woke up the grief was sitting there, waiting for me. I cried and cried, as if I was processing the loss for the first time. No doubt the looming prospect of saying goodbye to Jasmine was part of the reason for my emotion, but it was hard to believe how intense my pain was, given that it had been nearly seven months since I had lost Marty.

But this is what grief is like. One minute you can feel good and the next thing, the grief brings you to your knees.

Thankfully, I spent the next two weeks in the States with two very special women, both of whom allowed me to just be me. They let me do whatever I needed to do to deal with the sadness that would overwhelm me at any moment.

My first stop was Idaho, to visit my *mamacita*, Ruth Romero. I hadn't seen her for twelve years, but when I wrapped my arms around her at the airport it felt like no time had passed at all.

I had missed my special mentor, and it was a joy to be able to sit and talk with her for hours on end. At the age of eighty-two, she was such an inspiration—so fit, toned and healthy. She managed to be elegant while at the same time having a childlike sense of fun.

She shared so many insights about life with me, just like she always had.

'Lorraine, intimacy is not about sex; it is about penetrating each other's hearts,' she said during one of our chats. She was so right.

After a week with Ruth, I returned to LA to spend some time with Louise Calabro. We had been dear friends since 1986 when we both lived in Wellington. It doesn't matter how many kilometres separate us, we remain as close as ever.

Louie is warm and passionate and, like me, she loves the beach and shopping. We had so much fun together, and I laughed more in that week than I had in a long time.

Both Louie and Ruth looked after me gently, letting me be me—whatever that entailed. If I needed to have a nap or some quiet time on my own, I knew it was okay to do that. I could relax in their homes, safe in their unconditional love.

I didn't want to leave the States, but I had to. Yet again, when I walked through the door of my home I felt terrible. I started to have delusional thoughts, convincing myself that Marty was away on a trip and would be back soon. It was hard to shake this idea.

Fear seeped into my very being—*What am I going to do with my life? I have nothing left; my very existence has been taken away along with Marty.* I was a mess.

So I prayed and, as always, I heard God's voice. Don't fret, I was told. Know that everything is going to be okay. You will find your path again. Just keep moving.

In November, eight months after Marty died, I made a major decision: I was going to sell the house. I loved our home and it held years of happy memories, but there were many sad ones too. After coming back from Los Angeles, the truth hit me like a bat to the back of the head: the house was making me miserable. Every corner of it was filled with recollections of Marty and of us—painful reminders that there was no 'us' anymore.

I realised that being there wasn't helping me to move forward; it was holding me back. It was time to go.

Marty's counsellor, Didi Newcomb, helped me to see that

selling was the right decision. I had stayed in touch with her after Marty passed, and we talked about my feelings towards our home.

'There is too much sadness in the house and it makes things harder,' she wrote in a message to me. 'After the provision of familiarity and initial comfort, it has turned into a stark reminder of all you have lost.'

I started making a list of all the things I needed to do to get the house ready to put on the market. At the same time, Jasmine and Hilton were going through some tough times of their own, due to illness and injury. Trying to support them from afar while dealing with the house was stressful, and one night I woke up suffering a dreadful anxiety attack. My heart was racing and thoughts were bouncing around my head.

If Marty had been there he would have known how to calm me, but all I could do was stare at the empty side of the bed where he used to lie.

I prayed to God and asked my angels (Dad, Jean and Marty) to surround me with love and take my anxiety away.

Slowly but surely, a feeling of calm began to float through my mind and body, and my heart stopped pounding in my chest. I realised in that moment that all my constant worrying had to end. I have always been prone to fretting, but it was time to stop thinking negatively and start thinking positively. I know how important it is to stay in the present moment—to deal with the moment that is unfolding right now, rather than stressing about things that haven't actually happened.

It's okay, I told myself. *Hilton will be okay; Jasmine will be okay. You will be okay.*

I managed to go back to sleep and, after that night, I found it much easier to shut down my anxiety. Whenever I felt it encroaching, I would remind myself that this feeling was coming from my negative thoughts, nothing else, and I was able to halt the fear in its tracks. Reading Eckhart Tolle's book *The Power of Now* helped me a lot with this technique.

Marty had learned to control his anxiety during his illness, and that had been a huge breakthrough for him. Now it was my turn.

I hadn't been back from Los Angeles for long when I noticed that Air New Zealand had a sale on flights to Bali. I knew straight away that I had to go; it was my happy place, somewhere I would feel loved and supported. It would be the perfect place to spend time healing, and to work on the book I had decided to write.

The house was due to go on the market in February 2017, so I booked a two-month trip to Bali for the end of May, when hopefully everything would be settled. Now all I needed to do was get through the next few months.

Patricia and I did a meditation course at a Buddhist temple in Auckland, and that helped me immensely. It was a beautiful environment to meditate in, and during my first session I received a message from God. 'You are loved,' I was told.

It was amazing how sitting still and calming my mind could help me to hear the words I really needed.

Those close to me could see how much pain I was still in. At the end of November, nearly nine months after Marty passed, Patricia sent me a text.

'You are still struggling, and I know that despite your brave face and the steps that you make every day to "keep moving", it is still very hard for you. So I pray, and know that Marty and your angels and God are holding you in the palm of their hands and guiding you forward into the fullness of life once more.'

How wonderful it was to have a friend who truly understood what I was going through.

'Yes, my dearest friend, you know my struggle,' I replied to her. 'I do my best to put a smile on my face and to keep moving forward, but the truth is my heart is broken and I miss him so very, very much. The depth of sorrow I feel sometimes is as though Marty has only just left me, and it has been nine months now.

'Most mornings I wake and the room is so quiet, so still, and I feel so aware of Marty not being there and that I am on my own now. I shed tears, I pray, and then I pull the curtains open and face my day. For me, it is the hope that I will have a joyful heart again that keeps me going.'

That first Christmas without Marty, and the weeks leading up to it, were very difficult. Neither of my children was able to come home for Christmas—Jasmine was going to be dancing in Vietnam, while Hilton was playing rugby in Los Angeles. Emma would be spending Christmas with Marty's cousin Russell, who has been amazing since her papa died. He treats Emma like his own daughter, and it's beautiful to see.

While I was happy for our children, I felt a deep sadness about being without them on top of missing Marty, and I found myself dreading Christmas. In early December I wrote in my journal, 'Today I feel robbed.'

The physical feeling of grief was so strong that there were times when I could hardly move from weakness. But I made myself; there was no other choice.

Emma and I had a Christmas dinner together before she headed off to Russell's, and I gave her a charm Marty had picked out for her Pandora bracelet. As always, sharing a meal with Emma was a treat; I love spending time with her. I felt so proud of the way she was coping with her grief. It was very tough for her—after Marty died she found it hard to come to our home; he wasn't there and it reminded her of what she had lost. It was another sign for me that selling the house was the right thing to do.

Just before Christmas, I managed a trip to Melbourne to see Jasmine before she went to Vietnam. She was very busy with rehearsals so our time together was brief, and that was hard for me. I just wanted her all to myself! The fact that she was embarking on her first overseas job made me feel as if I was letting her go all over again, just like I had to do when she was sixteen. She had worked so hard for this opportunity and I was delighted for her, but I couldn't help feeling sad too. My baby was all grown up.

On the flight back to New Zealand, I wished that Marty was waiting for me at home so he could wrap me in his arms and hold me while I had a good cry.

Patricia invited me for dinner with her family on Christmas Eve, and it was a lovely evening; they welcomed me into their circle without hesitation. I spent Christmas Day with my parents, sisters and extended family, feeling grateful to be surrounded by their love. Thank God for technology—I had Skype calls with both Jasmine and Hilton, and it was such a gift to see their smiling faces.

I had chosen, when I woke up on Christmas morning, to be happy. 'I am blessed with my beautiful family, and I will cherish being with them,' I reminded myself.

My first Christmas without Marty was sad, but I had done so much grieving in the lead-up to the day that it wasn't as painful as I was expecting. That has been the case with most of the 'firsts' without Marty—first birthday, first Christmas, first wedding anniversary. I did a lot of my mourning before the actual event.

Valentine's Day 2017—which would have been our eighth wedding anniversary—was also the day the house went up for auction. It sold, with the settlement date in mid-May. I was pleased, and looking forward to downsizing to something smaller, perhaps a cosy cottage with lots of character.

Then, a week later, I had one of my bad days. The thought of having to start a new life on my own made me feel so weary. I loved my old life; I didn't want to have to begin again. But I had no choice.

The first anniversary of the day Marty departed came on 3 March. Dave, Patricia and Foxy joined me at home for a long lunch; Foxy bringing a special bottle of red wine that Marty had given him. We toasted our beautiful man and dear friend, and shared happy memories of him.

The closeness I have with Dave and Patricia is so strong that I have come to think of it as our 'Marty Love Bond'. It was one of the good things to emerge from what we went through: the three of us developed an unbreakable connection. It's important to recognise those positives and celebrate them.

I had started a gratitude jar after Marty passed: writing down the things I was thankful for on small pieces of paper and putting them in the jar. As I read through them on that first anniversary, it struck me again how lucky I was to have the love and support of family and friends.

Me and Emma at Adele's
Auckland concert.

At the end of March 2017, Emma took me to see singer Adele in concert. Russell knew Emma was a fan and had arranged for her to phone Adele. Emma was over the moon when Adele chatted with her and sent her five tickets! I felt so privileged that Emma chose me to have one of them; it was very thoughtful of her. The show was especially moving given that Adele was one of my and Marty's favourite performers. He would have loved it.

The settlement date for the house finally arrived. My belongings were moved into storage and I spent several days cleaning the house with the help of Marie, our lovely cleaner. Marie had been with us for ten years, right through Marty's illness, and I was going to miss her quiet grace and the love she had always shown us.

The day came to leave, and I couldn't help sobbing as I drifted around the empty house before closing the door behind me for the final time. It held so many memories. But I knew it was time to open new doors.

Jenny and Pope kindly offered me the use of the pool house behind their home until I was ready to find somewhere new. I made it feel like home with my favourite photos and other bits and pieces, and then I started preparing to go to Bali.

My family were worried about me going away on my own for two months, but I was convinced it was the right thing to do. The sadness I'd felt since Marty passed was relentless, and it was time to start healing my broken heart. I instinctively felt that a serene and spiritual place like Bali would be vital in helping me do that.

LOVE
WILL
NEVER
END

Chapter Twenty-five

From the moment you arrive in Bali, people smile at you. The customs officer who processed my arrival into the country was beaming, and I got a huge grin from the driver sent to collect me from the airport. I smiled back—even though he was half an hour late and I had been starting to worry about him.

He drove me to Ubud, where I was spending the first thirty days of my two-month stay. It was dark when I arrived, so I didn't fully appreciate the beauty of my surroundings until the next morning. I'd been looking for somewhere with a traditional Balinese feel in a natural environment, and I struck gold with the Villa Beji Indah. It's small, with just eleven rooms, and is set in a lush tropical rainforest.

The staff were wonderful—gentle and kind, and constantly smiling. They made me feel safe, cared for and loved, and their energy was exactly what I needed. I wasn't in Bali to just laze around; I had to heal my broken heart.

It was time to strip back the layers that I had built up around me over the four and a half years since Marty's diagnosis. I needed to find answers to the important questions: who was I now, and what was I going to do with my life?

I spent my days practising yoga, swimming, exploring Bali and writing this book. I had to get the balance right; it would have been completely draining if I had devoted too much time to examining my life. Writing could be exhausting; some subjects

Me with staff members from the Villa Beji Indah, who looked after me so well in Bali. I gave them a cake to thank them for their kindness.

more than others. It was fun reliving my days on *Dancing with the Stars*, but going back over the past four and a half years was tough, and I had moments of deep grieving as I tapped out the words. Sometimes I just had to close my laptop and step out into nature, letting its energy and beauty refresh my soul.

Being Marty's caregiver, especially in that last year, had involved a lot of responsibility. With that came a feeling of heaviness that had stayed with me, and I needed to shake it. I felt sure that time alone in such a deeply spiritual and peaceful place was helping me do that.

I could feel Marty's presence, and he kept showing me signs he was there. Everywhere I looked I saw the colour orange, his colour. On my first day a taxi arrived to take me into Ubud township, and I opened the car door to find bright orange seats. I couldn't help laughing.

'Okay, honey, let's go,' I said.

In a café a few days later, a trip to the bathroom took me past a staircase where flowers were arranged to spell out the words 'Love will never end'. The flowers were, of course, orange.

And it seemed for my entire stay, I was surrounded by orange butterflies. It was comforting, knowing Marty was there with me.

When the teacher at one of my yoga classes in Bali asked my name, I gave him Marty's nickname for me, Raine.

'You are abundance,' he told me.

He also had some advice for me. 'You are in your head too much and you need to be in your heart more.'

Well, that was most definitely true!

The Balinese people are spiritual and intuitive, and they're known for their healing abilities. One morning I woke up feeling like crap, and I decided to go and see Made Lunas, a healer who had been recommended to me. I'd had very little sleep after a night spent listening to a rat running around in the roof of my room—rats are my least favourite thing and I am petrified of them. I was exhausted, and I figured the time had come to see the healer.

My two-hour session with Made was incredible, filled with

truth and wisdom. He told me that since Marty's passing, I had closed the world out. It was time to open myself up again to living with a happy heart, not a sorrowful one.

Made said that Marty didn't want me being sad anymore.

'He wants to see you thrive,' Made told me.

When I heard that, I thought, *Of course he does.* Marty loved me; he would not want me to be miserable. In that moment I made a conscious decision that I would seek happiness. I would not let missing Marty drag me down.

I left the healing session feeling as if a heavy weight had been lifted from me. I decided on a new mantra: 'I will have a happy heart and I will have a happy face.' I still remind myself of that mantra every day.

Bali had more healing experiences to offer me. Later in my stay I visited Ida Resi Alit, Bali's youngest high priestess. I had heard that during a near-death out-of-body-experience in 2007, when she was twenty-one, Ida received instructions from the divine being and woke in a higher state of consciousness, able to perform special mantras and rituals. She was suddenly so accomplished in these ancient spiritual arts that she was put through a painstaking process of examination and rigorous physical tests, before being ordained as a high priestess of Hindu Dharma, the main religion in Bali.

Ida is revered for her wisdom and knowledge, and presides over many profound religious ceremonies, including a water purification blessing.

Her name kept coming up, so I sought out one of her ceremonies. I quickly saw that Ida is a very special person. She moves like a gliding swan but what struck me most was her voice—I have never been so transfixed by a voice.

The spiritual ceremony involves Ida sitting on her knees, chanting and ringing a bell (for an hour and a half; I don't know how she kept it up) and then pouring blessed water over people.

When my turn came, she asked me and the people alongside me to feel our hearts deeply, and we became very emotional. The water felt so good, and she told me to keep wiping it over my face and hair. We were encouraged to move our feet, moan out loud and 'let it all go'.

'Feel your heart, go deeper, let it go,' Ida whispered softly in her beautiful voice.

This part of the ceremony continued for about five minutes and felt amazing. Emotions that had been buried deep inside me were being released; I could feel it happening even after the blessing had ended. I felt *free*. I'd had a lot of negative energy stored, and it was good to get it out.

I was very blessed to have this experience. After the healing session with Made and the ceremony with Ida, I knew there had been a shift in my heart. The two healers had helped me move in a positive direction, and I began to feel more ready to reconnect with the world. Instead of being broken, I was growing stronger and preparing for the next step.

During my time in Bali I stayed in Sanur, Jimbaran and Seminyak as well as Ubud. Although I was on my own most of the time, there were opportunities to meet up with a handful of people I knew, including Louise Calabro, who happened to be visiting Bali from Los Angeles. Louie and her family were staying an hour's drive away, but they made the effort to come and see me on my fifty-third birthday. Being able to hug Louie on my birthday was a wonderful gift. I was also glad to have the company of my lovely sister Jenny for my final week in Bali.

The other person I caught up with was my acupuncturist and spiritual mentor, Peter, who lives in Sanur with his gorgeous wife Josephine and their adorable son Rayner.

Peter and I had an in-depth discussion about the fact that we all handle grief differently. People who are not so connected to their hearts on a conscious level can find it hard to support someone like me. I told Peter that only a few people had kept in contact with me since Marty's death, apart from our very close friends. Whenever I bumped into a friend of Marty's who hadn't been in touch they would often apologise, saying they'd been busy and had been wondering how I was.

When this happened, I would stop them halfway through what they were saying and gently put a hand on their arm.

My dear friend Louise Calabro is a beach lover just like me. This photo was taken on another occasion in LA.

'It's okay, I know you have been busy, and thank you for thinking of me,' I would say. I could tell how awkward they felt.

Peter wasn't surprised. 'The reason people don't visit you, Lorraine, is that they can't handle your grief. They find you too scary. For some people, it is easier to push grief down and not face it; it's too confronting.'

I could understand this. I do feel sad for those who choose not to go deeper and connect with how they are truly feeling—not just when it comes to grief, but when it comes to love. Having a heart-to-heart connection with another person, like the one I had with Marty, is a beautiful thing.

I watched Marty with his friend Dave, and they had that kind of deep bond. I know Marty wanted to achieve that with some of his other loved ones, but not everyone was emotionally available on that level. It was sad that he didn't get to do that.

Marty and I connected not only on a heart-to-heart level, but on a soul-to-soul one as well. This means allowing the other person to see everything about you. There is no judgement, just unconditional love given and received. It is absolutely blissful.

I try to connect with people on a deeper level now, and I consider it to be a legacy from Marty. Peter agreed that it was Marty's gift to me. It is one I will always be grateful for.

I came back to New Zealand from Bali a different person in many ways. My healing had definitely begun and, although I have more work to do, I had taken the first steps on my journey to finding out who I am—and feeling joy in my life again.

Before I went to Bali I felt very cocooned; I was protecting myself because I wasn't ready to face people. But once I stepped off that plane at home I felt safe to start opening myself up again. I had gained a lot of confidence.

I can talk much more easily about Marty now. Jenny and Pope had friends visiting recently who didn't know about Marty's death, and one of them said something about my husband.

'Lorraine's husband passed away last year,' Pope said quickly.

Pope's friend said he was sorry.

'It's okay,' I replied, and I meant it. The pain is not as piercing as it once was. I think I can put that down to the healing work I have done, as well as the passing of time—time really is a great healer. When I look back to how I felt a year ago, the difference now is quite incredible. And I know that next year will be better.

If there's one thing I'd like people to understand, it's that grief is a different experience for everyone. You need to let someone who is mourning the loss of a loved one deal with it in their own way. It is their grief, not yours.

> 'The grief was so intense that it drained me. But it could also be beautiful, because it was a reflection of the incredible love I shared with Marty.'

For me, in those first months after Marty passed, grief was an onslaught of overwhelming sadness that I couldn't control. It started deep in the pit of my gut and rose right up through my body to my heart, which felt as if it was going to explode with the weight of love and loss. My mind and body were flooded with a deep sadness and a longing for Marty's physical presence.

Something as simple as a song we both loved could set off the grief—the tears would start rolling down my cheeks and I couldn't stop them. I would be consumed by the reality that Marty was no longer here on earth and part of my life. The grief was so intense that it drained me. But it could also be beautiful, because it was a reflection of the incredible love I shared with Marty.

I think of my grief as coming in waves. Sometimes those waves are huge and terrifying; on other days they are small but choppy. Then there are gentle waves that lap against the sand, and the times when the water is still and peaceful.

You don't always know when grief is going to strike, and you can't usually stop it. But you do have a choice about how long you let it stay. Sometimes it feels right to let the grief sit with you for a while; it's almost as if you need to feel it. But you also need to know when to close the door on it, and get moving again.

I miss Marty so much. I will grieve for him for the rest of my life. Because I loved him so deeply, his loss will be a part of me forever. Grief is the price we pay for love.

But my grief has changed, and it sits in a different place now. It used to be right in front of my face; now it is just behind me. It will always be there, but it doesn't confront me the same way it did.

I was asked recently if I thought I would love again. I don't know if I will, but I do hope so. I believe in love, and I like the idea of sharing my life with someone special.

But do I want to find a soulmate? No. I've had my soulmate. I believe that the type of connection Marty and I had only comes once in a lifetime. Any future relationship will be different to what Marty and I shared, and that's okay. I am not looking for something the same. I feel lucky to have had what we had.

One of the lessons I have learned from life—and particularly from my journey with Marty—is that there are some things you just can't control. I had always been a bit of a control freak, but when Marty got diagnosed it finally sank in: things happen that you cannot change, no matter how desperately you want to.

Losing this controlling trait was good for me; it made me a much more relaxed person. I think I became more empathetic and compassionate, and I definitely grew spiritually and emotionally because of what I went through. I changed for the better.

I have been able to find positives in what happened. Yes, I would have given anything to change the situation and have Marty here with me still, but I don't, and I have to accept that. Finding the good things that have come out of it helps to ease the pain.

For a while there I felt that I had lost myself, but I now have a better sense of who I am. I know what matters and what doesn't. I am still unsure what the future holds for me workwise, but I trust that something will happen to lead me down the right path. I would love to be able to inspire other women in some way; I'm hoping I will find something that allows me to do that.

There were times when I felt it was too hard to stay here without Marty, but I can see now that my life has to go on. He didn't have a choice, but I do, and I choose to live what is left of my life with joy. I have a lot of living to do yet; I am still young. I can't wait to be a grandmother for starters.

There's a passage by Oriah, one of my favourite authors, that really resonates with me:

'When I imagine myself as an old woman at the end of my life and ask myself how I will evaluate my time here, there is only one question that concerns me: Did I love well?'

It's important to me to be able to answer 'Yes, I did love well.' And I can say that thanks to Marty.

I am truly thankful to my beautiful man for what he gave me in our time together. I treasure the lessons I have learned about life, loss and love, and I would be delighted if sharing them helps others.

Love is what life's all about. We should be grabbing the chance to love whenever we can. Love will always find a way to make everything okay—I have found that out first-hand.

There are still bad times; those moments when the grief grips me and my heart hurts so much. When that happens, I try to feel Marty's love, and I remind myself that he doesn't want me to be sad.

I hear that lovely voice saying, 'Just keep moving, Raine, keep moving.'

I am, Marty. I am.

Captions and credits for chapter opening images

Chapter One (pp. 10–11) Me as a young girl in that classic shy pose with my head on the side. Spot the sticking plaster on my knee!

Chapter Two (p. 24) Posing on the beach after winning the 1983 Miss Mount Maunganui title.

Chapter Three (p. 38) Miss Universe 1983. My swimsuit was purple with sparkles sewn into the bodice.

Chapter Four (pp. 52–53) My *mamacita*, Ruth Romero, accompanied me on several of my trips as Miss Universe; meeting elephants was a highlight. Photo by Bernard Jordaan.

Chapter Five (p. 66) Waving to the audience at an event leading up to the 1984 Miss Universe pageant, where I was to crown the new winner.

Chapter Six (p. 82) One of my favourite shots from the time I spent modelling in Sydney. Photographer unknown.

Chapter Seven (p. 96) Fun times with Hilton and Jasmine on the trampoline. I have always adored being a mum.

Chapter Eight (pp. 110–111) Me and Jasmine enjoying a catch-up at a café.

Chapter Nine (p. 124) Marty and I knew the time was right for us when we met up again in 2005.

Chapter Ten (pp. 138–139) Performing the cha cha with Aaron Gilmore in my very first live show for *Dancing with the Stars*. You can see in my face how nervous I am. Photo by Neil Mackenzie.

Chapter Eleven (p. 158) My sister Carolyn and her daughter Claudia were so brave throughout Claudia's cancer treatment. Photo by *NZ Woman's Day*.

Chapter Twelve (p. 168) Our wedding day was filled with so much love. The wedding photos were taken by Todd Eyre and Ross Coffey for *The Australian Women's Weekly*.

Chapter Thirteen (p. 180) One of my all-time favourite modelling shots, which was taken for a Living Nature campaign. Photo by Monty Adams.

Chapter Fourteen (p. 196) Mum and I joined forces to work with the Breast Cancer Foundation.

Chapter Fifteen (p. 210) Marty and Jasmine share a moment together. Our family became even closer after Marty's diagnosis.

Chapter Sixteen (p. 224) I am proud of the young woman that Jasmine has become. Photo by Monty Adams for the *New Zealand Woman's Weekly*.

Chapter Seventeen (p. 234) Frances Jones was one of the friends who gave me loving support throughout Marty's cancer journey.

Chapter Eighteen (p. 244) Marty and Hilton with New Zealand cricketers Ross Taylor (left) and Martin Guptill. Marty thought of them as the sons he never had.

Chapter Nineteen (p. 254) Emma could always make Marty's eyes light up. Photo by the *New Zealand Woman's Weekly*.

Chapter Twenty (pp. 266–267) Dinner with Jasmine and Emma at a favourite Indian restaurant. Marty was suffering by this time but he always made an effort for our girls.

Chapter Twenty-one (p. 276) Emma and Marty striking a pose on Christmas Day 2015. Marty came downstairs that morning dressed in his white wedding suit with an orange shirt.

Chapter Twenty-two (p. 288) Emma marvelling at the monarch butterfly that landed on Marty's flowers on the day after his funeral. Marty had told us to keep an eye out for monarchs.

Chapter Twenty-three (p. 298) Taking time to reflect after Marty's passing.

Chapter Twenty-four (pp. 308–309) Me and Hilton on a trip to Queenstown in the months after Marty passed. We came across this wooden seat with its gentle reminder of what's important in life.

Chapter Twenty-five (p. 322) The flower arrangement that I stumbled upon at a café in Bali. The blooms were bright orange: Marty's favourite colour.

Me with my loving support crew in 2017: sisters Carolyn, Sue and Jenny and our mum Glad.